New Retro

GIORGIO PESCE · JORGE PEZ · GEORGES POISSON · GEORG FISCH · GEORGE FISH · JORGEN FISK · BORBE RIBA · YORGOS PSARI · JORGE PEIXE ⊚

ATELIER

MÉDAILLE
D'OR
LISBONNE
1994

160 g
POIDS NET

INGREDIENTS:
POISSON, SEL,
HUILE VEGETALE

POISSON

Giorgio Pesce

ATELIER POISSON
AVENUE DE MORGES 33   1004 LAUSANNE·SWITZERLAND
TEL +41 21 · 311 59 60   FAX +41 21 · 312 12 48
POISSON@ATELIERPOISSON.CH

A CONSOMMER DE PREFERENCE AVANT LA DATE LIMITE

New Retro

Classic Graphics, Today's Designs

Brenda Dermody
Teresa Breathnach

With 655 illustrations, 588 in color

Thames & Hudson

Acknowledgments The authors are indebted
to the following people for their assistance with
bringing this book to fruition:

The designers, studios and individuals who
contributed material to this project. Without their
generosity and enthusiasm there would be no book.

For reading and commenting on the text, Clare
Bell, Kieran Corcoran, Alison Fitzgerald, Suin
Hanrahan and Linda King.

For assistance with research, David Dabner,
Steven Heller, Michael Hope, Greg Kindness,
Linda King, Elaine Lustig Cohen, John McMillan,
Freda Sack and Jim Stoddart.

Austin Carey for his above and beyond creative
input throughout this project.

The Faculty of Applied Arts Research Committee
at the Dublin Institute of Technology; John
O'Connor, Head of the School of Art, Design
and Printing; Kieran Corcoran, Head of the
Department of Design at DIT for their support.

Jacket design Austin Carey, Brenda Dermody
Book design Austin Carey, Brenda Dermody
Picture research Teresa Breathnach,
Austin Carey, Brenda Dermody, Sarah Jameson
Original book concept Angela Patchell

First published in 2009 in hardcover in the United
States of America by Thames & Hudson Inc.,
500 Fifth Avenue, New York, New York 10110

thamesandhudsonusa.com

First paperback edition 2010

Library of Congress Catalog Card Number
2009902030

ISBN 978-0-500-28846-7

Printed and bound in China by Imago

Contents

Introduction:
What Is Retro Design?

Our experience of rapid change in all areas of life expresses itself as a need to buy, wear, look at, live in and listen to a variety of recent and distant pasts. Almost as soon as products, images, materials and techniques become defunct, we treat them as a reservoir of endlessly recyclable and reusable ideas. Historians describe how the close relationship between graphic design, the conditions that surround it and the need to communicate leave it best placed to express the zeitgeist of an era (Meggs, 1998). It is ironic, then, that one of the most important and abiding aspects of our own zeitgeist is the sampling of historical forms themselves.

Looking at a range of examples, this book asks: what is retro design? In tandem with an almost seamless absorption of stylistic influences like classicism or Swiss typography, there is a more self-conscious referencing of particular styles, motifs, techniques and materials in design. The term *retro* has been in use since the 1970s to describe this sort of appropriation (Woodham, 2004; 1997). Although the retro label often brings to mind the revival of mid-century modern styles that occurred from the 1980s and 1990s onwards, this book shows that designers now embrace an eclectic variety of styles, motifs, techniques and materials drawn from their own historical ragbags. But a fascination with old styles is not in itself a new thing. Designers throughout the 19th and 20th centuries all borrowed freely from other eras. Placing our own interest in the context of a history of revivalism allows us to see that each period recalls the past according to its own needs and experiences.

Historicism in Design The 19th century saw Owen Jones's *Grammar of Ornament* (1856) use the latest technology to present a detailed categorization of a whole range of ornamental styles, including those drawn from the past. By this time, the profusion of styles available to manufacturers and printers alike catered for eclectic popular taste. In this context, the revival of past styles might be understood as both an affirmation of the new technologies that could produce them, and a reaction to the rapidity of change which such technologies brought about. The latter emerged as part of a wider climate of reform in the decorative and applied arts, which sought to overturn the indiscriminate and often overwhelming use of decoration in manufacturing. The art critic John Ruskin was highly influential in this regard. In *The Seven Lamps of Architecture* (1849) and *The Stones of Venice* (1851), Ruskin saw the revival of both the Gothic style and the system that produced it as a way forward for contemporary design, linking the reduction in status of the individual craft-worker with the decline of standards in decoration. His ideas were taken up by the Arts and Crafts movement, whose leading proponent, William Morris, looked to the medieval world for both a means of production that would improve the lot of the worker and stylistic models that would satisfy the need for a reformed use of ornament. The Kelmscott Press,

Opposite **Barbara Jones,
Black Eyes & Lemonade
poster, UK, 1951** Designed
by Barbara Jones, this poster
promoted the exhibition 'Black
Eyes & Lemonade: British
Popular Art' held at the
Whitechapel Art Gallery in
London. The exhibition was
organized as part of the Festival
of Britain and in the same
year that Jones's book *The
Unsophisticated Arts* was
published. The poster was
overprinted in black on yellow,
using a decorative 19th-century
typeface. The smaller text
radiating out from the eyes
lists the popular art forms and
objects on display.

established by Morris in 1891, sought to redress the loss of quality
in contemporary books by reviving past approaches to book design
and production. In America, Frederick Goudy's Camelot Press was
involved in a similar revival, alongside the Merrymount Press, Roycroft
Press and Wayside Press. Indeed, the influence of the private-press
movement was widespread and continues to be felt to the present day.

From the turn of the century onwards, the dominant motivation
among designers was to turn away from historicism in a bid to find
new forms suitable for a new world. However, the past as an inspiration
was never entirely absent. Popular advertisements produced in the
first two decades of the 20th century used Gothic, Baroque and
Rococo motifs to lend new products artistic (Heller and Lasky, 1993),
and perhaps socio-historical, legitimacy. Although Henry Ford is
associated with the introduction of modern systems of production,
he also demonstrated his interest in a popular taste for the historical
or the traditional by establishing Greenfield Village in Michigan, a
development matched by the setting up of Colonial Williamsburg in
the same period. Both were forerunners of contemporary heritage
attractions. Despite the focus of many designers on the development
of a modernist approach, there is evidence of consumers' continued
interest in the application of both indigenous and more exotic
historicist styles to a range of products: inter-war Britain, for example,
saw the return of a taste for mock Tudor furniture which emphasized
cultural stability (Woodham, 1997), and the Art Deco or Moderne
style of the same period integrated new forms with both classical
and Egyptian motifs. Alongside modernist disdain for the endless
recycling of older models, classicism remained an influence for some.
Typographers like Rudolf Koch and, later, Jan Tschichold, also found
inspiration in the history of their discipline. Koch produced several
typefaces based on historical models for the Klingspor foundry,
including *Neuland* (1923), which evoked early woodcut printing.
Although Tschichold was central to the development of the new
typography, he later looked to a sensitive use of historical precedent.
Eric Gill's *Perpetua* typeface for the Monotype Corporation (1925) was
based on the monumental capitals found on Trajan's Column in Rome
(*c.* AD 114), and he also embraced the new directions provided by a
study of medieval manuscripts, incunabula and the work of the type
founders John Baskerville and William Caslon (Meggs, 1998).

The drive to look forward rather than back remained the dominant
vision in the 1950s and 1960s, but it is clear that there was a continued
interest in both established traditions and historicism. A resurgence
of interest in traditional crafts can be seen in the publication of Charles
Marriott's *British Handicrafts* (1945) and Margaret Lambert's *English
Popular and Traditional Arts* (1946), designed and illustrated by Enid
Marx, and in Barbara Jones's exhibition 'Black Eyes & Lemonade:
British Popular Art' (1951) at the Whitechapel Art Gallery, London.
Abram Games's work for the Festival of Britain (1951) used designs

"BLACK EYES & LEMONADE"

A FESTIVAL OF BRITAIN EXHIBITION BY ARRANGEMENT WITH THE ARTS COUNCIL

BRITISH POPULAR ART

AND IN CONJUNCTION WITH THE SOCIETY FOR EDUCATION IN ART

WHITECHAPEL ART GALLERY

Barbara Jones

AUGUST 11th – 1951 – OCTOBER 6th

Daily 11-8 :   Sundays 2-6 :   Closed Mondays :   Nearest Station Aldgate East

Shenval Press London and Hertford

that drew on the 19th-century slab-serif Egyptian type styles of the type founders Figgis, Thorne and Austin, alongside more modern forms, at the behest of the Festival's typographic committee (Aynsley, 2004; Heward, 1999). The interest in 19th-century graphic forms continued throughout the later 1950s and 1960s and was extended to include popular styles of typography and imagery of the 1920s and 1930s. The reappearance of versions of 19th-century types contributed to this revival in America: the Morgan Press reissued versions of Victorian wood-types, while Photo-Lettering, Inc. issued *Psychedelitypes* (1968), a catalogue of new faces based on similar models. The application of photocomposition to typesetting during the 1960s allowed for greater flexibility in the selection and arrangement of type styles and sizes, perhaps promoting a thirst for the new. Psychedelia of the 1960s incorporated influences drawn from Art Nouveau as well as popular graphics and other cultures. The resulting designs of Victor Moscoso, Rick Griffin, Alton Kelley, Stanley Mouse and Wes Wilson developed an entirely contemporary visual language designed to appeal almost exclusively to their young American audience, communicating a sense of belonging to a counter-culture. Similarly, the growth of youth culture in Britain necessitated new styles to set it apart from the Establishment. John McConnell's logo for Barbara Hulanicki's Biba boutique (1963) displayed the influence of Art Nouveau, and the display lettering for other shops used bright colours and exuberant faces drawn from folk art as well as Victorian display types (Aynsley, 2004). This climate of experimentation was also represented by the development of an underground press which employed the IBM Selectric typewriter for arranging text and offset lithography to print it. Richard Neville, the Australian founder of *Oz*, touched on the relationship between such methods of production and the appropriation of a wide range of historical and other forms when he said that '… a photographic process enables sweeping visual versatility, so the whole world can be plundered for decoration – from food labels, oriental comic books, Tibetan scrolls and *Encyclopaedia Britannica*. Copyright is ignored' (Aynsley, 2004). In America, designers associated with the Pushpin Studios looked to typographic and illustrative Victoriana, Art Nouveau and Art Deco or Moderne – Seymour Chwast's *Artone* type (1963) evoked French Art Nouveau models, and Milton Glaser's *Babyteeth* (1966) drew on lettering of the 1920s and 1930s. Paul Davis's painting style looked to primitive American Colonial art, and Barry Zaid embraced popular graphic styles of the 19th century.

The influence of the Pushpin approach continued to be felt in the following decades, when the next phase of revivalism began. Paula Scher, Louise Fili, Carin Goldberg, Daniel Pelavin and Lorraine Louie are all associated with the revivalist impulse of the late 1970s and 1980s. Britain's Malcolm Garrett, Peter Saville and Neville Brody also looked to the past to create work with a rather different flavour. This phase saw designers being inspired by modernist works of the 20th century, often attracting significant criticism. Elements associated with a vernacular visual language also acted as a springboard, particularly throughout the 1980s and 1990s – Tibor Kalman, Charles Spencer Anderson, Art Chantry, Joe Duffy and Michael Mabry all evoked popular visual forms in their work. The last two decades have seen designers quoting directly from specific works, referencing particular historical periods as pastiche or parody; layering such references (e.g. psychedelia, which in itself references Art Nouveau), being influenced by specific approaches to the design process, creating a general sense of the past through nostalgic effects or demonstrating a concern with expressing the peculiarities of the vernacular and of historical printed ephemera. This current passion for past styles among designers is matched by a return of interest in the decorative and the handmade.

Thus a history of revivalism in design demonstrates that our own era is not unique in the appropriation of past forms. Also clear, however, is that each period recalls the past according to its own aesthetic, social, economic and technological experiences. Our relationship to the past has its own contours, whether it relates to our motivations for using it, the particular pasts we look to or the ways in which we use them.

So what is it that motivates designers and consumers alike to embrace revivalism, and what are the implications of this for our relationship with the past?

Critiquing Retro As well as a whole range of individual reasons and experiences, several broad-based factors contributed to graphic designers embarking on revivalism as a way of working. For example, from the 1980s onwards the emergence of design history as a discipline in its own right was important, particularly when it became a formal aspect of design education, while increased access to earlier work must also have been afforded by the publication of several illustrated histories of graphic design, other offerings of the graphic-design press and the activities of professional organizations. The development of the computer as a design tool made experimentation with typefaces and layouts easier, while the advent of the World Wide Web increased access to work from the past.

The context most frequently cited in discussions of historical or other forms of appropriation in contemporary design, however, or indeed in relation to any popular engagement with the past, is that of Postmodernism. While modernism resulted from a production-oriented world view concerned with the successful communication of a message, Postmodernism focuses on the consumer, calling on him or her to play an active role in the deconstruction of the message. Graphic designers working in this vein '… no longer [search] for a single message or visual form but instead [use] hybrid imagery, mixed typographic styles and [delight] in complex composition' (Aynsley, 2004). The appropriation of past styles also became a central component of Postmodern graphic design, as did the use of the vernacular (Heller and Lasky, 1993; Poyner, 2003). Much of the discussion of retro-styling in graphic design is informed by broader critiques of Postmodernity. Indeed, one of the classic texts heralding the emergence of Postmodernism was also instrumental in turning our attention to everyday graphics as objects of interest. Robert Venturi, Denise Scott Brown and Steven Izenour's *Learning from Las Vegas* (1972) looked to vernacular signage as a source of interest.

The emergence of this phase of revivalism in graphic design generated a great deal of debate, mirroring the response to the rise of the heritage industry and a widespread turn to nostalgia. One of the principal arguments against the eclectic revivalism we have witnessed has been that much work is at worst a stultifying and parasitic plagiarism, and at best a pastiche, both suggesting a dearth of real creativity and firmly identifying our own era as the 'age of plunder' (Savage, 1999). Critics have argued that the search for endless novelty and the importance of simulacra have resulted in a form of retrievalism which belittles or ignores the original meaning of such styles and appeases an apparently endless appetite for the novel and the different. Ultimately, designers are seen to participate in the creation of an apparently hollow or depthless image that often simply appeals to an escapist search for nostalgia as a panacea for modern-day ills. Nostalgia in design can even be associated with bad taste (Sparke, 1987). In their use of graphic forms associated with the styles and clip art of the 1940s and 1950s, some designers were charged with the production of a false sense of nostalgia using 'jive modernism' (Kalman *et al.*, 1994). Clearly, the issues of plagiarism or lack of innovation in design, or the idealization of the past and the reduction of its meaning by treating it as a product, are very real concerns. However, although valuable, such a perspective may not acknowledge the full complexity of this appropriation. Are there other ways of seeing our engagement with the past in or through graphic design than as an escapist response to the present and a creative dead end?

The Appeal of the Past The debate surrounding our use of retro-styling continues to expand. We might even understand revivalism as an alternative way of knowing the past to formal historical enquiry (Samuel 1994; Guffy 2006). Like the nature of revivalism itself, the arguments that surround it are not straightforward. There is complexity in both our creation of design works and our consumption of them. Several issues might affect these processes. Different designers and different audiences create different sets of meanings when they participate in revivalism. For example, our own cultural, gender and generational identities, as well as a whole host of other experiences, surely have an impact on our reading of retro work. Drawing on a specific period of America's past may produce a different set of meanings there than in Britain or Japan, for example, and the use

Opposite **Milton Glaser, *Mahalia Jackson* poster, US, 1967** Milton Glaser's poster for a Mahalia Jackson concert at the Lincoln Center in New York shows a silhouette of the renowned gospel singer and Glaser's own Art Deco-inspired typeface *Babyteeth*. Despite this inspiration, the poster is unmistakably 1960s in feel.

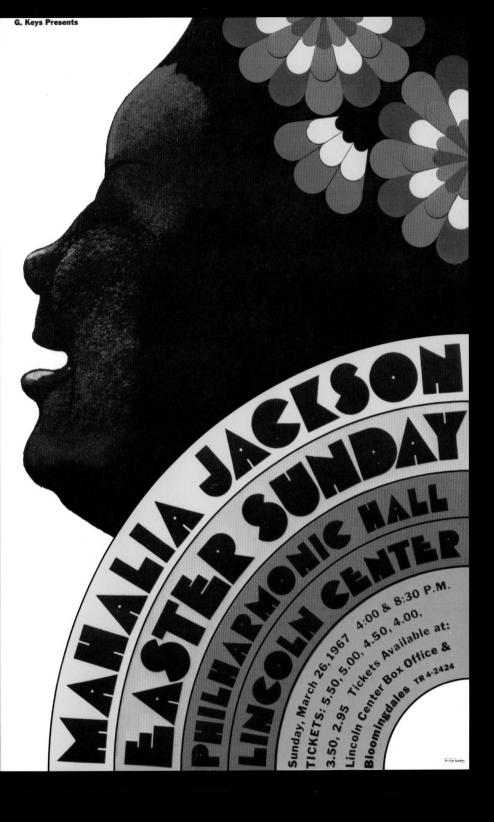

MAHALIA JACKSON
EASTER SUNDAY
PHILHARMONIC HALL
LINCOLN CENTER
Sunday, March 26, 1967   4:00 & 8:30 P.M.
TICKETS: 5.50, 5.00, 4.50, 4.00,
3.50, 2.95   Tickets Available at:
Lincoln Center Box Office &
Bloomingdales TR 4-2424

of Soviet symbols may hold different meanings for those who lived through the Cold War than for those who did not. We might argue that the reuse of styles associated with other times can be entirely appropriate, depending on both the client and the content in question. Indeed, in a business in which the principal goal is to communicate, the adoption of symbols and a visual language that is understood by the intended audience may be unavoidable. Related to this is the question of why the revival of particular styles seems to emerge at specific times: the availability of particular sources, the formative experiences of a particular generation of designers or consumers, or the meaning of a specific style in the context of the needs of a whole society might all interact to encourage their use.

The quotation of works or styles from other eras can become a powerful form of parody which can be both witty and subversive, as well as a factor that sets any current revivalist impulse apart from others (Guffy, 2006). The past is a particularly fruitful field for this type of commentary, as the distance between then and now allows such alternative readings to emerge. This type of reflexivity is at the heart of a shift which has seen design and other artistic fields turning the spotlight on their own disciplines. The concept of reflexivity implies that we are active participants in dealing with our own experiences of the external world by using the systems it offers rather than being passively blown hither and thither by them. Exploring this concept further might extend our understanding of why and how designers and consumers alike continue to turn to the past in their creation and use of graphic design.

Although the private-press movement has been active for over a century, the last decade has seen a particular revival of interest in traditional printing techniques. This involves both the rediscovery of these techniques and the reproduction of the aesthetic associated with them using contemporary technology. It is perhaps no accident that such a revival has coincided with the dominance of the computer as a design tool. On the part of designers, the depiction of both the effects and the tools of letterpress printing may indicate simple nostalgia or perhaps a more complex search for a lost authenticity in the creative process, associated with tacit or hands-on knowledge. This is particularly so in the case of promotional or other materials aimed at designers themselves, and may relate to the growth of reflexivity in the discipline, as discussed earlier. Clearly designers and their clients must respond to the desires of their audiences, and the renewal of such techniques must be understood in this context, too. The availability of digital fonts that reproduce the visual effects of letterpress type has surely contributed to its use as one of many design devices feeding a search for nostalgia among consumers.

But what does this aesthetic mean to them? The desire to capture a 'look' of nostalgia may be fuelled by a sense of dissatisfaction with the present. It can be understood as a useless search for a past that never was or, alternatively, as a way of mounting an active critique of modern life using the means that are immediately accessible to us (Tannock, 1995). In this context, it is likely that consumers also read such devices as indicating authenticity, lending the message, cause or product being promoted a similar 'truth', whether it deserves this status or not. This may mean that we are passive dupes of consumerism, but it may also be that we are actively expressing our discontent in one of the only contexts readily available to us in everyday life. We are not necessarily trying to reconstruct the past but to create an alternative present (Jens, 2005). One of the main areas in which historicist styles are used is in the promotion of food and drink, where strategies that appeal to childhood memory, the pursuit of comfort and domestic ideals abound. Our own concerns about production processes and their effect on the quality of products are clearly important factors here. We might also ask to what extent class or cultural identities play a role in this appeal (Weiss, 2004).

The concept of authenticity might also be applied to a range of other visual devices now used to evoke a sense of the past. This might encompass the reproduction of actual artefacts of graphic ephemera or the effect of oldness, as opposed to their use as sources of stylistic inspiration. An analysis of this type of design may be revealing in terms of consumer thirst for history, or memory, in a tangible form, and extends our understanding of popular interaction with the past more generally. Most of us have felt the legacy of a lived-in book, the humanity of the bus ticket that marks the place of a previous reader, or the appeal of an old postcard once exchanged by strangers. Our experiences of these things are not only visual, but often involve touch, smell and sound: in an age of electronic communication, tactile forms can offer an important experience for the consumer which goes beyond the retrieval of information (Barrett, 1997), perhaps prompting both actual and imagined memories (Kwint *et al.*, 1999; Barrett, 1997). Like those on old buildings or furniture, the marks of age that printed artefacts display might be considered as patination, an indication of all that the artefact, and its users, have experienced (Lash and Urry, 1994; Lowenthal, 1985). Such an auratic quality may appeal to us as a way of accessing a sense of the past directly, immediately and intimately. We may be attracted to items of printed ephemera because of their status as temporal witnesses which help us to root our own experiences. Like the use of devices that suggest authenticity, it may be that it doesn't matter to consumers that the actual objects they are handling are fake, as the feeling they induce may be very real indeed. Could it be that our consumption of an old-style package may allow us to feel that we are living an alternative everyday life, if only momentarily?

We can only touch on the range of meanings that might be bound up in our use of the past here, and we cannot do complete justice to the complexity of arguments and concepts that surround it. We hope, though, that revisiting some concepts and raising new ones as

Above and opposite **Cahan Associates, Adaptec annual report, 1996** In order to simplify the content and make it more accessible, Cahan Associates created this annual report for an IT company in the style of a 1940s children's book. The artwork was shot in overlays from the original ink drawings to more closely echo book-production methods from the period. The resulting design generated huge media interest at the time. The report was featured on the cover of *USA Today*, and interviews with principal Bill Cahan were broadcast on the major American news networks.

This book belongs to

ABC&D

A CORPORATE BOOK

See Molly at work.
She is doing all the things
that Wally is trying to do.
Only she does them better.

Molly has an Adaptec host
adapter and SCSI peripherals.
See Molly multitask. From her
PC to peripherals, and even to
her network, she really works fast!

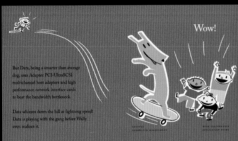

But Data, being a smarter than average
dog, uses Adaptec PCI-UltraSCSI
multichannel host adapters and high
performance network interface cards
to beat the bandwidth bottleneck.

Data whizzes down the hill at lightning speed!
Data is playing with the gang before Wally
even realizes it.

Wow!

No problem! Molly can configure her laptop with
Adaptec's PCMCIA host adapter and EZ-SCSI
software. And that will connect her with all kinds
of peripherals. Now Molly can do research on the
Internet, share files, make faxes and save her
homework from anywhere! Even from Space!

John C. Adler
Chairman of the Board

F. Grant Saviers
President and Chief Executive Officer

Molly is very smart.
She is first in her class.
She dreams of going to
the moon. Just one
thing worries Molly...
her homework is due
in the morning.

See Wally hard at work.
He tries to scan big photo files.
He tries to move video files
to his backup drives.

Poor Wally. Wally thinks his new
processor makes him work faster.
He does not know that the data
link between his PC, peripherals,
and the network is more critical.

possibilities might encourage others to expand on them, or indeed to counteract them completely. Proper empirical examination of particular situations will eventually provide a far more in-depth and nuanced discussion of retro design. Unless we understand specific instances of revivalism in greater depth, how can we comment in a meaningful way about the field as a whole? We must also broaden our reflections on retro-styling to see them alongside other forms of popular engagement with the past. We do not negotiate graphic design in isolation but rather in a state of glorious interaction.

A selection of the best of retro design is drawn together here in a stimulating portfolio of new work. From projects that have embraced a fundamental approach to design to those that reinterpret style, materials and techniques, this book shows how graphic designers now reference the past to produce new and dynamic visual forms. Our focus is largely on work produced since 2000 as our objective is to give a clear sense of the current state of play. We have not aimed to provide an exhaustive survey of the genre but have endeavoured to include work that is representative of designers' own broad-ranging approaches.

Without wishing to dilute its meaning, links and crossovers between retro and other elements of the contemporary design scene lend further interest to much of the work included here. At its best, graphic design now is recalling its past to create something new and exciting in the present.

References

_Aynsley, J., *Pioneers of Modern Graphic Design: A Complete History,* London, 2004

_Barrett, T., 'The Future of the Book as Viewed from inside a Tornado', in Bierut, M., W. Drenttel, S. Heller and D. K. Holland (eds), *Looking Closer 2: Critical Writings on Graphic Design*, New York, 1997

_Guffey, Elizabeth E., *Retro: The Culture of Revival*, London, 2006

_Heller, S., and J. Lasky, *Borrowed Design: The Use and Abuse of Historical Form*, New York, 1993

_Heward, T., 'Revivalism and Cultural Shift: British Graphic Design since 1945', *Design Issues* 15/3, 1999, pp. 17–33

_Jens, H., 'Sixties Dress Only! The Consumption of the Past in a Retro Scene', in Palmer, A., and H. Clark (eds), *Old Clothes, New Looks: Second Hand Fashion*, Oxford, 2005

_Kalman, T., J. Abbott Miller and K. Jacobs, 'Good History / Bad History' (1991), reprinted in Bierut, M. (ed.), *Looking Closer: Critical Writings on Graphic Design*, New York, 1994

_Kwint, M., C. Breward and J. Aynsley (eds), *Material Memories*, Oxford, 1999

_Lash, S., and J. Urry, *Economies of Signs and Space*, London, 1994

_Lowenthal, D., *The Past Is a Foreign Country*, Cambridge, 1985

_Meggs, P., *A History of Graphic Design*, New York, 1998

_Poynor, R., *No More Rules: Graphic Design and Postmodernism*, London, 2003

_Samuels, R., 'Retrochic', in *Theatres of Memory*, London, 1994

_Savage, J., 'The Age of Plunder' (1983), reprinted in Bierut, M., J. Helfland, S. Heller and R. Poynor (eds), *Looking Closer 3: Critical Writings on Graphic Design*, New York, 1999

_Sparke, P., *Design in Context*, London, 1987

_Tannock, S., 'Nostalgia Critique', *Cultural Studies* 9/3, 1995, pp. 453–64

_Weiss, E., 'Packaging Jewishness: Novelty and Tradition in Kosher Food Packaging', *Design Issues* 20/1, 2004, pp. 48–61

_Woodham, J., *A Dictionary of Modern Design*, Oxford, 2004

_Woodham, J., *Twentieth Century Design*, Oxford, 1997

Retro Elements

The history of graphic design is a journey through technological, scientific and cultural change. Throughout the last century, the limitations and possibilities presented by technology have been combined with social and aesthetic concerns to produce designs distinctive to their own eras and cultures. Type, image, materials, techniques and colour have all played a part in the development of these visual languages. They have acted as powerful tools, both attracting attention and coding information in the communication of messages and ideas.

The designs shown on the following pages illustrate this process, from the impact of mechanized printing technologies of the nineteenth century through to modernist reassessments of the representation of word and image in the early twentieth century, and on to the return to the decorative from the 1960s onwards. The ways in which visual devices are recycled underpins our responses to retro work, calling up associations with the past in a very immediate way. Such devices can be used to suggest specific eras, to test our associations with them or as springboards for the creation of new approaches to the problem of visual communication. One thing is certain: the meanings generated by the reuse of historical references will always be both new and redolent of their own times.

1850–1918 Mechanization and Reform

1.1	**1765**	**1796**	**1800**	**1801**	**1814**	**1815**	**1816**	**1821**	**1827**
Mechanization and Popular Print	sand-casts the first display lettering	Aloys Senefelder invents lithography	Lord Stanhope invents his cast-iron printing press	John Gamble's paper-making machine	Friedrich Koenig's steam-powered cylinder press	Vincent Figgins publishes type specimens, including the new *Antique*, or *Egyptian*, and *Tuscan*-style faces	William Caslon IV publishes the new Grotesque face *Two Lines English Egyptian* – the first sans serif type	William Thorowgood's *New Specimen of Printing Types* showing Robert Thorne's fat-face types	Darius Wells invents the lateral router, a machine for the manufacture of large wood-types; Applegath and Cowper's steam-powered multiple-cylinder press

1892	**1897**	**1.2**	**1851**	**1861**	**1882**	**1883**	**1884**	**1887**	**1888**
The American Type Founders Company is established	Tolbert Lanston's Monotype machine	The Arts and Crafts Movement	Great Exhibition of the Industry of All Nations in London. Ruskin publishes *The Stones of Venice* (following *Seven Lamps of Architecture*, 1849)	The company of Morris, Marshall and Faulkner is established	A. H. Mackmurdo establishes the Century Guild in London	Mackmurdo's *Wren's City Churches* appears	Art Workers Guild is established. Emery Walker advises Century Guild on design of the *Hobby Horse* journal	Selwyn Image's 'On the Unity of Art' essay published in *Hobby Horse*	The Arts and Crafts Exhibition Society is formed, with Walter Crane as its president. Charles R. Ashbee establishes Guild of Handicraft. William Morris designs *Golden* type

1.3	**1886**	**1891**	**1893**	**1894**	**1895**	**1896**	**1897**	**1898**	**1899**
From Art Nouveau to Proto-modernism	Eugène Grasset's first poster	Toulouse-Lautrec's *Moulin Rouge* poster	Aubrey Beardsley's *Le Morte d'Arthur*. First edition of *Studio* is published, featuring the work of Beardsley, Jan Toorop and Henry van de Velde. Talwin Morris joins Blackie's publishing house in Glasgow as art director	William Nicholson and James Pryde establish Beggarstaff Brothers agency. Will Bradley begins the *Inland Printer* journal covers. Oscar Wilde's *Salome* is published, with illustrations by Aubrey Beardsley. Jan Toorop's *Delftsche Slaolie Salad Oil* poster	Samuel Bing establishes L'Art Nouveau Gallery in Paris. Herbert MacNair and Macdonald sisters produce *Glasgow Institute of Fine Arts* poster. Will Bradley's poster for the *Chap Book*	Charles Rennie Mackintosh produces *The Scottish Musical Review* poster. Théophile Steinlen's poster for *Affiches Charles Verneau*. Beggarstaff's poster for *Don Quixote* at the Lyceum Theatre in London	Vienna Secession is formed	Alphonse Mucha's poster for *Job Cigarette Papers*. *Ver Sacrum* magazine is published. Gustav Klimt's poster for the first Vienna Secession	Henry van de Velde's *Tropon Food Concentrate* poster and packaging

1834

William Leavenworth combines the pantograph with the lateral router so new wood-types can be produced with greater ease

1837

Queen Victoria begins her reign. German Godefroy Engelmann patents the chromolithographic process

1839

Louis-Jacques Daguerre presents innovative Daguerreotype prints to the French Academy of Sciences. William Henry Fox Talbot presents his ideas on photogenic drawings, or photograms, to the Royal Society

1843

The first Christmas card is produced

1844

Fox Talbot's book *The Pencil of Nature* is published

1846

Richard M. Hoe perfects the rotary lithographic press

1851

The Great Exhibition of the Industry of All Nations in London's Hyde Park

1856

Owen Jones's *Grammar of Ornament* is published. Louis Prang establishes his chromolithographic printing company in the US, producing popular graphics typical of this era including greeting cards

1886

Ottmar Mergenthaler's Linotype machine

1888

The Kodak camera is manufactured for the first time

1891

Kelmscott Press produces more than fifty titles between 1891 and 1896

1892

William Morris produces *News from Nowhere*

1893

Morris designs *Chaucer* typeface

1894

Morris produces *The Story of The Glittering Plain*, illustrated by Walter Crane. Frederick Goudy establishes Camelot Press

1895

Goudy designs *Camelot* typeface

1896

Morris designs *The Works of Geoffrey Chaucer*, illustrated by Edward Burne-Jones. Morris dies. Ashendene, Eragny and Vale presses are established

1898

Walter Crane's *The Bases of Design* is published

1900

Emery Walker and T. J. Cobden-Sanderson establish the Doves Press

1902

Essex House press produces the *Essex House Psalter*

1923

Goudy establishes the Village Letter Foundry

1900

Walter Crane's book *Line and Form* is published. Otto Eckmann's *Eckmannschrift* typeface

1904

Josef Hoffman and Kolomon Moser establish Wiener Werkstätte

1905

Lucien Bernhard's *Priester Matches* poster

1907

Peter Behrens joins AEG in Germany and produces logo. Deutscher Werkbund is formed

1910

Behrens's AEG *Metallfadenlampe* poster

1915

Alfred Leete's *Kitchener Wants You* poster

1916

Hans Rudi Erdt's *U Boote Herhaus!* poster

1917

James Montgomery Flagg's *I Want You for the US Army* poster. Julius Gipken's *Deutsche Luftkriegsbeute* poster for an exhibition of captured enemy aircraft

1.1

Mechanization and Popular Print: Typography

This period is characterized both by great technical and industrial progress and by reactions to it. Elaborate decoration could be produced more quickly and cheaply than ever before, and both manufacturers and consumers revelled in a profusion of decorative styles. This era saw the introduction of a wide variety of typefaces, the use of photography and the printing of colour images. The range of graphic material available to the consumer expanded hugely, changing everyday experiences of modern life. This included everything from illustrated periodicals and books to advertisements and packaging.

Visual Elements

– Reliance on letterpress typography, sometimes combined with woodcut or wood-engraved imagery

– Variety of styles, weights and sizes of type in one piece

– Large display and decorative types

– Horizontal / vertical layouts and texture dictated by letterpress technique

– Restrained use of colour

Right **The Siege of Troy, or, The Giant Horse of Sinon, poster, UK, 1833** The 1830s saw the introduction of several technological innovations that were employed throughout the century. This poster for Astley's equestrian performance shows the lively use of display types. The inventive play of decorative, high-contrast fat face and antique or Egyptian letterforms and printers' ornaments is particularly characteristic of the period, as is the printed surface produced by the letterpress process itself. The visual variety created by type is strengthened by the striking use of woodcut imagery.

Below right **Alastair Keady, Wornwood, typeface, UK, 1990** As a student at the Royal College of Art in London, Alastair Keady worked with the letterpress facilities housed at the rear of the Victoria & Albert Museum. When the press was moved in 1990 to a smaller space, there was no longer room to house much of the college's letterpress collection. Keady decided to make a usable archive of one specific wood-type face, which was not going to survive the move: 'The provenance of the face I chose is unknown, but it was a fairly typical 19th-century Grotesque in capitals only. The font was available in limited quantities, but mostly very worn through decades of use and abuse. After printing off sample runs of full sets of each character, the best and worst impressions were scanned and redrawn digitally. Worn characters were assigned to uppercase keys, while the less-worn characters were assigned to lowercase. The intent was to give a passable impression of the real thing, retaining some degree of character variance.'

Opposite **W. S. Johnson, Vauxhall Gardens Final Masquerade, poster, UK, 1859** Letterpress-printed posters and broadsheets were the principal means of communication during this period, and typography was key. The sand-casting of display lettering, the introduction of the iron printing press, the development of machinery for the production of large wooden display type, and a taste for ornament drawn from a variety of cultural and historical sources all had an impact on the look of the era.

Responding both to the competition posed by lithographic technology and to the constraints posed by their own discipline, letterpress printers sought to capture the attention of consumers by manipulating styles, weights and sizes of type. This poster typifies the unrestrained exuberance of the era as type foundries produced more and more new styles. The printer here used both the popular slab serifs in plain and italic forms, and a sans serif face. Sans serifs were a style of letter characterized by heavy rectangular serifs. They had first been used as early as 1816, perhaps as a variation of an Egyptian face with the serifs removed, and initially for descriptive, or body, text. By the 1850s, they were being given more importance, different foundries producing versions known as Grotesques, Dorics and Gothics. Here the word *masquerade* was produced as a wood engraving.

VAUXHALL GARDENS.

UNDER THE HIGH PATRONAGE OF HER MOST GRACIOUS MAJESTY.

FINAL
MASQUERADE

Will take place at these Gardens.

THIS EVENING, THURSDAY, SEPTEMBER 8,

On a scale of great splendour, when every available advantage, which this long-celebrated Scene so abundantly affords, will be made use of.

The ROYAL GARDENS will be BRILLIANTLY ILLUMINATED.

Mad^{lle} CAROLINE'S EXERCISES !

Signor BOLTARI,

THE ITALIAN DEVEL RIDER,

Amongst other Entertainments, a GRAND

VOCAL CONCERT

Will be given, which will be assisted by Mrs. H. P. Grattan, Miss Betts, Mr. Allen, Mr. S. Jones, &c.

DUCROW'S POPULAR AND CLASSICAL SCENES OF THE CIRCLE

Presenting the EQUESTRIAN WONDERS of

Sig^r ANTONIO BOLTARI—Mr. HICKEN—Mr. STICKNEY.

The Feats of the Grotesques, and Exercises of Arena, commencing with Mr. HICKEN, in his Pantomimic Delineation on a Single Horse at full speed, and in his admired Seven Characters, entitled

Triumph of Fame, or, Lifes Sports & Characters

Delineating Tar of all Weathers, Paul Pry, Bavarian Broom Girl, Vanderdecken the Flying Dutchman, and Fame, bearing his Circlet of Victory, Glory!

Sig^r ANTONIO BOLTARI, the great Italian Devil Rider, will make his seventh appearance in England, in his extraordinary and novel act of Horsemanship, as

The VOLTIGEUR OF MILAN

Or THE WILD HORSEMAN!

Mr. STICKNEY, the popular American Equestrian, will give his graceful Act of Horsemanship and Lofty Leaping, as the OMPLYIC SPRINGER.

THE SCENES VARIED BY THE DROLLERIES OF THE GROTESQUE, Mr. FULLER.

Riding Masters, Mr. WIDDICOMB, and Mr. NEEDHAM.

The Scenes of the Circle will be varied by the high training and sagacity of the Diminutive Steed FIREFLY, in a Characteristic Scene, as the Black Pony Chingring Merrybell.

Quadrille and Character Dances, as given at Her Majesty's Bal Costume.

A NEW BALLET DIVERTISSEMENT, IN WHICH

LA PETITE TAGLIONI

Will introduce LA CACHUCHA DANCE and LA TARENTELLA.

NUMEROUS GROUPS OF BALLERINES AND CORYPHEES,

In original and varied Costumes, will exhibit many Characteristic Processions & Dances under the direction of

Mr. W. H. PAYNE, of Covent Garden Theatre.

LES ORCHESTHES DE LA DANSE

Will be conducted by that Eminent Professor, MONSIEUR COLLINET; and A MILITARY BAND will be stationed in the Grounds, to perform alternately with them, under the direction of Mr. BADDELY.

FIREWORKS,

By that celebrated Artist, Mr. DARBY.

Herr JOEL, and other Artists of Talent and Celebrity, are engaged to gratify the Company.

An elegant SUPPER, with superior WINES, will be provided as usual, in the Gardens, without any increase of Prices upon the Vauxhall Carte.

Masks, Dominos, and Fancy Dresses, may be had at Obbard's Masquerade Warehouse, No. 3, Tavistock Street, Covent Garden; at Simmonds's Warehouse, 72, Castle Street, Leicester Square; opposite Bear Street; and Mrs. Fenton's, Opera Establishment, 79, Strand; and also of her, at the entrance of the Gardens.

Tickets paid for last Thursday the 1st instant, will be admitted this Evening.

Gentlemen's Tickets, 7s. 6d. Ladies' Tickets, 5s.

Which may be obtained at Mr. Andrews's Library, 167, New Bond Street; Bailey's Library, 158, New Bond Street; Mr. Sams's Library, St. James's Street; Mr. Ebers', Mr. Hookham's, and Mr. Mitchell's Libraries, Old Bond Street; Mr. Seguin's Library, 13, Regent Street; Mr. Boubourg's, Cafe Françoise, Haymarket; Mr. Bailey's, Bookseller, Cornhill; Mr. Obbard's Masquerade Warehouse, 3, Tavistock Street, Covent Garden; Mr. Simmonds's Warehouse, 72, Castle Street, Leicester Square; Mr. Nathan's, 19, Castle Street, Leicester Square, opposite Bear Street; and Mrs. Fenton's, 79, Strand, with whom an arrangement has been made for the hiring of Dresses

DOORS WILL BE OPENED AT NINE O'CLOCK.

W. S. JOHNSON, Printer, Soho.

1.1

Mechanization and Popular Print: Colour and Image

One of the principal achievements of the age was the development of chromolithography. Although colour had been introduced to printed imagery prior to this, either by hand or through a variation of the woodcut process, chromolithography represented a reliable and economic way of reproducing colour images for a large audience and heralded a new departure in the popular visual experience. For both producers and consumers alike, colour came to signify progress, a leitmotif of the age. The discovery of the first synthetic dye, a bright mauve, by William Henry Perkin in 1856 and its consequent cheap manufacture prompted a craze for this colour in particular among Victorian consumers.

Visual Elements

- Inspired by an eclectic variety of historical and geographical sources, along with the possibilities presented by technology and popular taste

- Free-form, hand-drawn lettering integrated with imagery

- Elaborate ornament and sentimental imagery

- Use of unrestrained full colour through the technique of chromolithography

Right **Huntley & Palmers Christmas Cakes, catalogue page, UK, 19th century** Although perhaps a little saccharin and exaggerated to our eyes, the complexity of colour achievable through chromolithography must have seemed impressively naturalistic to the Victorian consumer. This new technique involved analysing original coloured images and reproducing them using several lithographic stones. When overprinted, these gave the appearance of a full range of colours. Owen Jones used this new colour technology to reproduce his influential *Grammar of Ornament* (1856), which helped to fuel the Victorian love of elaborate and eclectic decoration.

Below right **P22 Font Foundry, *Victorian Swash*, typeface, 2000** Designed as part of a set for the Albright Knox Art Gallery's exhibition in Buffalo, New York of the work of the 19th-century artist James Tissot, *Victorian Swash* was influenced by a Victorian typeface called *Columbian*.

Opposite **Bailey Rawlins' *Expanding View of the Great Exhibition*, UK, 1851** The Great Exhibition expressed the optimism and confidence of the age. The swirling ribbon and acanthus-leaf motifs on this souvenir of the event reflect the popularity of profuse ornament: visitors to the exhibition would have seen such decoration applied to the whole gamut of exhibits there, from domestic furniture to industrial machinery. Although this piece is partly hand-coloured, the printer has drawn attention to his progressive use of colour lithography in a deft piece of self-promotion. Both social and technological developments had also seen the range of graphic ephemera available to the consumer expand. Such ephemera frequently showed the sentimental imagery so dear to the Victorian mind, like the sheets of printed 'scraps' with which scrapbooks, screens and other items were adorned by accomplished young ladies. The thirst for novelty was also demonstrated by techniques like die cutting to emphasize already elaborate imagery.

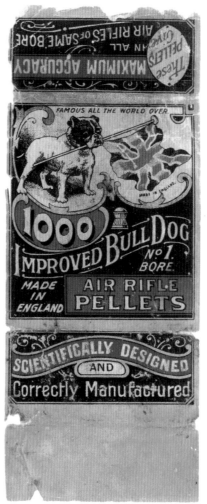

Left **1000 Improved Bulldog Air Rifle Pellets, label, UK, c. 1900** The emerging fields of branding and advertising embraced the seamless integration of colour, imagery and lettering offered by the lithographic technique. No longer constrained by the linear nature of typesetting, hand-drawn lettering could follow any shape or style. Advertisements and packaging often used imagery that would appeal to nationalistic tendencies. This package combines two popular symbols of Britishness, the Union Jack and the bulldog. The product was associated with progressive manufacture and science, and with qualities of tenacity and bravery, through its use of word and image in a typically ornate style.

Below **Linotype,** *Thorowgood*, **typeface based on a 1953 revival of the original, UK** This typeface was first cut by Robert Thorne but was released in 1836 by William Thorowgood, who had purchased Thorne's foundry in London in 1820. This digital version is the 1953 revival of the face.

Opposite left **Mixed pickles by Crosse & Blackwell, UK** *Opposite centre* **Warner's Safe Cure for Kidney and Liver and Bright's Disease, bottle and label, UK** *Opposite right* **Pure Lucca Oil by Crosse & Blackwell, UK, all** *c.* **1879** The advent of prepackaged items meant that packaging played an important role in convincing buyers of a product's quality during the 19th century. The mechanization of the glassmaking industry had already enabled the introduction of moulded lettering on bottles, and although such techniques may have signified progress to their original consumers, it is perhaps the imperfections produced in their manufacture or through the process of ageing that appeal to us.

Qa abcdefghijklmnopqrstuvwxyz ABCDEFGHIJKLMNOPQRSTU VWXYZ 0123456789

1.2

The Arts and Crafts Movement

The Arts and Crafts movement attempted to counteract what were perceived as the aesthetic and moral ills induced by industrialization, including the mechanization of the printing process. Looking to the Middle Ages for inspiration, William Morris and others were active in encouraging the private-press movement with the aim of reviving the crafts of fine printing and book production. Carefully conceived type, ornaments and illustrations were beautifully printed on handmade paper and bound into impressive volumes: the antithesis of contemporary book production. The private-press movement continued to develop throughout the 20th century, and the Arts and Crafts movement had a far-reaching influence on design generally.

Visual Elements

_ Inspired by medieval manuscripts and early printed books

_ Blackletter, or Gothic, and Roman typefaces with ornamental initials

_ Use of Pre-Raphaelite figures and patterns using natural forms

_ Letterpress type with woodcut illustrations and ornament

_ Restrained use of colour

_ Fine materials

_ Solidity, simplicity and harmony

Right **Monotype's *Goudy Oldstyle*, typeface based on Frederick Goudy's typeface of 1915** Designed for American Type Founders, this typeface shows Goudy's attention to detail in several unusual characteristics. These include the use of diamond-shaped dots with a calligraphic feel on the lowercase 'i' and 'j', and in the full stop, colon, semi-colon and exclamation and question marks. Morris Fuller Benton later added bold and extra-bold versions of the face.

Below right **Linotype's *ITC Golden Type*, typeface based on William Morris's *Golden* typeface of 1892** Designed by Sigrid Engelman, Andrew Newton and Helga Jörgensen in 1989, *ITC Golden Type* revived Morris's original Arts and Crafts typeface for the Kelmscott Press. Morris based his design on Nicholas Jensen's Venetian letterforms of the mid-15th century, and the letters were cut by the punchcutter Edward Prince.

Opposite **William Morris and Edward Burne-Jones (Kelmscott Press), page showing type and illustration from *The Works of Geoffrey Chaucer*, UK, 1896** Morris established the Kelmscott Press in 1891, and *The Works of Geoffrey Chaucer* is regarded as one of the press' finest books. It exemplifies Morris's commitment to achieving unity in design by displaying continuity and balance in layout, as well as by matching text, ornament and illustration in style, texture and weight. Serious study of early printed books and manuscripts provided Morris with a wealth of inspiration. The typeface used here is *Chaucer* (1892) and was based on the Blackletter hand used in German manuscripts of the medieval period. Edward Burne-Jones's illustrations are in a romantic Pre-Raphaelite style, while the densely patterned ornament used in borders and around decorative initials shows stylized natural motifs. Both illustrations and ornaments were produced using the woodblock process, while the type was produced using the letterpress technique.

Morris's aim was not to devise a pastiche of past styles but to create wholly new works in the tradition of fine book production. He was not averse to using the most progressive technology of the day to produce the results he required. He used photography both to enlarge examples of early type so that he could study the letterforms in detail and sometimes to transfer designs for illustrations to woodblocks for cutting. His types were machine-cast, and initials that were to be repeated were printed using electrotypes, an industrial process that produced a harder printing surface that did not degrade as quickly.

Although this work may appear heavily ornate to us, it represented a well-planned alternative to the indiscriminate eclecticism of the commercial printing of the era. Its association with the earthy quality of the handmade contrasts with the sophisticated slickness of modern-day production techniques.

abcdefghijklmnopqrs
tuvwxyzABCDEFGH
IJKLMNOPQRSTUV
WXYZ 0123456789

Ff

abcdefghijklmnopqrs
tuvwxyzABCDEFGH
IJKLMNOPQRSTUV
WXYZ 0123456789

Qq

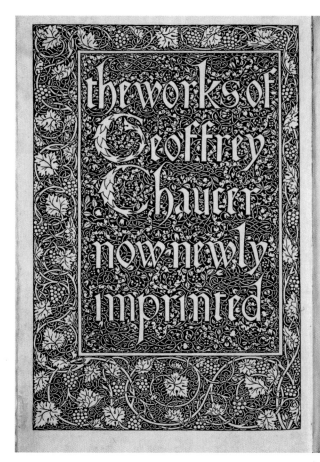

the works of
Geoffrey
Chaucer
now newly
imprinted

HERE BEGINNETH THE TALES OF CANTER-
BURY AND FIRST THE PROLOGUE THEREOF

WHAN THAT Aprille with his shoures soote
The droghte of March hath perced to the roote,
And bathed every veyne in swich licour,
Of which vertu engendred is the flour;
Whan Zephirus eek with his swete breeth
Inspired hath in every holt and heeth

The tendre croppes, and the yonge sonne
Hath in the Ram his halfe cours yronne,
And smale foweles maken melodye,
That slepen al the nyght with open eye,
So priketh hem nature in hir corages;
Thanne longen folk to goon on pilgrimages,
And palmeres for to seken straunge strondes,
To ferne halwes, kowthe in sondry londes;
And specially, from every shires ende
Of Engelond, to Caunterbury they wende,
The hooly blisful martir for to seke,
That hem hath holpen whan that they were
seeke.

BIFIL that in that seson on a day,
In Southwerk at the Tabard as
I lay,
Redy to wenden on my pilgrym-
age
To Caunterbury with ful devout
corage,
At nyght were come into that hostelrye
Wel nyne and twenty in a compaignye,
Of sondry folk, by aventure yfalle
In felaweshipe, and pilgrimes were they alle,
That toward Caunterbury wolden ryde.

1.3

From Art Nouveau to Proto-modernism

The Art Nouveau style emerged at the end of the 19th century, heralding an entirely new visual language for graphic design. Combining Rococo, Symbolist and Japanese influences, it is characterized by its emphasis on line and its abstraction of natural forms. One form of Art Nouveau was predominantly curvilinear, while its counterpart was rectilinear.

Visual Elements

_ Inspired by nature, Symbolist painting and Japanese art

_ Free-form, hand-drawn rather than letterpress types

_ Integration of type and image

_ Focus on line: either sinuous and curvilinear or grid-like and rectilinear

_ Organic forms and motifs, and use of attenuated figures

_ Flat, two-dimensional shapes and asymmetrical layouts

_ Lithography and chromolithography

Right **Henry van de Velde, *Tropon*, Poster, Germany, 1897** Henry van de Velde's work for Tropon's processed egg white has become an iconic example of the style, and represents the application of a new set of artistic ideas in a commercial environment. Departing from naturalistic representation, Van de Velde used abstract forms and colour to suggest the product. His approach built on the widespread interest in expressing the force of growth, the creation of two-dimensional patterns of negative and positive space, and the strength of line as a primary component. The integration of the brand name was achieved here by allowing the descenders of the letters to follow the line of the image.

Opposite left **Alfred Roller, *Secession*, poster, Austria, 1903** Roller's exhibition poster for the Vienna Secession sees the replacement of imagery with letterforms. The distinctive attenuated style of lettering used for the word *Secession* is shown against a background of geometric shapes suggestive of wallpaper or textile designs, and is offset by the equally abstracted block-like letterforms used in the rest of the poster, a favoured device of Austrian Art Nouveau. Rudolf von Larisch, a teacher at the School of Applied Art in Vienna, was influential in this regard for both the Vienna Secession and the Wiener Werkstätte that followed. He advocated the exercise of filling a square with a letterform, thereby training the artist to consider both positive and negative space and take a controlled approach to the use of letters. The long and narrow format, two-dimensional forms and geometric shapes are also typical of this era, matching the aims of the Secession in creating a new visual idiom for the 20th century.

Opposite right **Linotype's *Eckmann*, typeface after Otto Eckmann's original of 1900** Typefaces were often highly ornamental, matching the whiplash lines and organic curves of the images that accompanied them. Eckmann produced several typeface designs for the Klingspor foundry in Offenbach, including *Eckmann*. This face was drawn with a brush rather than a pen, and its forms were influenced by a combination of Japanese, medieval and Roman references. This and other Art Nouveau faces mark a clear departure from the solidity of the letterpress display lettering we associate with the 19th century.

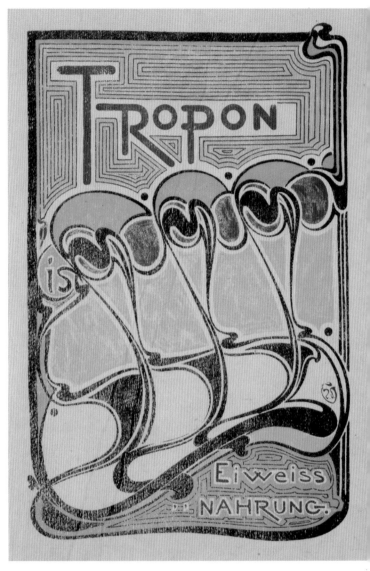

abcdefghijklmn
opqrstuvwxyz
ABCDEFGHIJKLN
OPQRSTUVWXYZ
0123456789

Aa

Right **Monotype's** *Bernhard***, typeface based on Lucian Bernhard's** *Bernhard Antiqua* **typeface of 1912** Bernhard is best known for his *Plakatstil* posters, a style of advertisement that depicted products in a reductive manner using blocks of flat colour. He designed *Bernhard Antiqua* in 1912 for the Flinsch foundry in Frankfurt-am-Main. Further weights of the face were produced by the Bauer Type Foundry in the 1920s.

Opposite **Aubrey Beardsley, cover of** *The Yellow Book***, UK, 1894** The heady years of the 'Yellow Nineties' took their name from the cover of the literary journal *The Yellow Book*. Often associated with a bohemian lifestyle, Beardsley's distinctive illustrations were used on several of the journal's covers, contributing to its avant-garde image. However, he resigned as art editor after only four issues because of an alleged association with Oscar Wilde, following Wilde's infamous trial. Beardsley depicted grotesque figures using a delicate line, balancing blocks of solid black and white with intricate patterns. These were reproduced using the photographic black-and-white lineblock process.

abcdefghijklmn
opqrstuvwxyz
ABCDEFGHIJKLMN
OPQRSTUVWXYZ
0123456789

Ff

The Yellow Book

An Illustrated Quarterly

Volume III October 1894

Price
$1.50
Net

London: John Lane
Boston: Copeland & Day

Price
5/-
Net

2.1

Early Modernism and Avant-garde Experimentation

1897
Stephan Mallarmé publishes his poem *Un Coup de des*, using typography and space to suggest meaning

1909
Filippo Marinetti publishes *Manifesto of Futurism*

1910
Marinetti drops 800,000 copies of his Futurist leaflet *Against Past – Loving Venice* from a Venetian clock tower onto crowds below

1913
The Futurist journal *Lacerba* is first published. Kasimir Malevich's Suprematist painting *Black Square*

1914
World War I breaks out

1915
Marinetti's Futurist poem *Montagne + Vallate + Strade X Joffre* published; Man Ray becomes interested in Dadaism

1917
De Stijl movement is founded in Holland and the journal *De Stijl* begins publication. Cabaret Voltaire is opened by Hugo Ball in Zurich. The periodical *Dada* begins publication. Revolution in Russia

1918
Guillaume Apollinaire publishes his poems *Calligrammes* in which typography creates images

2.2

European Modernism and the New Typography

1916
Edward Johnston's *Railway* typeface

1918
Johnston's London Underground symbol first appears

1919
Walter Gropius founds Weimar Bauhaus. Bauhaus manifesto is published using Lyonel Feininger's *Cathedral* woodcut

1920
Paul Klee joins Bauhaus

1922
Kandinsky joins the Bauhaus. Oskar Schlemmer designs second Bauhaus symbol

1923
Moholy-Nagy replaces Johannes Iten at Bauhaus. 'Staatliches Bauhaus' exhibition held in Weimar. Herbert Bayer's design for Thuringian State Bank notes. Hendrik Werkman begins to produce typographic experiments called Druksels, and issues *The Next Call* journal

1925
Bauhaus moves to Dessau. Herbert Bayer designs *Universal* alphabet. Jan Tschichold's *Elementare Typographie* is published

1926
Heinz Schulz-Neudamm's *Metropolis* poster. William Addison Dwiggins joins

1928
Dr Mehemed Fehmy Agha becomes art director of *American Vogue* and, later, *Vanity Fair* and

1929
A. M. Cassandre's *Bifur* typeface. W. A. Dwiggins designs *Metro* typeface for Linotype

1930
Jean Carlu produces covers for *Vanity Fair*

1931
Cassandre's *L'Atlantique* poster

1932
Cipe Pineles joins Condé Nast as designer under Agha

1934
Alexey Brodovitch is made art director of *Harper's Bazaar*

1935
Joseph Binder moves to New York. Franklin Roosevelt's government initiates the

1936
Egbert Jacobson becomes director of design at the Container Corporation of

1920

Victory for Red Army of the Bolsheviks in Russia

1921

Man Ray moves to Paris and becomes involved in Surrealism. Vladimir Tatlin and Aleksandr Rodchenko denounce Art for Art's Sake and turn to design for everyday life. El Lissitzky becomes involved with De Stijl, Dadaism and the Bauhaus. Russian journal *Vesch* begins publication

1922

Dadaist periodical *The Bearded Heart* is published. Kurt Schwitters, Van Doesburg and Kate Steinitz create *The Scarecrow Marches.* Aleksei Gan's *Konstruktivism* is published

1923

Dadaist journal *Merz* begins publication. Ilya Zdanevitch's poster for the play *Part of the Bearded Heart.* Lissitzky designs the poetry book *For the Voice.* Rodchenko designs magazine *Novyi Lef*

1924

Lissitzky and Schwitters collaborate on issue of *Merz. The Isms of Art 1914–1924* edited and designed by Lissitzky

1925

Van Doesburg's book *Grundbegrisse der neuen Gestaltend,* designed by Moholy-Nagy, is published

1927

Fortunato Depero's *Depero Futurista* is published

1932

Man Ray's *London Transport Keeps London Going* poster

1935

John Heartfield's *Adolf the Superman* poster

1927

Paul Renner designs *Futura* typeface

1928

Jan Tschichold publishes *Die Neue Typographie.* Gropius, Moholy-Nagy and Herbert Bayer leave Bauhaus. Rudolf Koch designs *Kabel* typeface. Piet Zwart designs *catalogue for the Nederlandsche Kabelfabriek (NKF) company.* Gerd Arntz begins to produce *isotype* pictograms. Eric Gill designs *Gill Sans* type. Fortunato Depero moves to US, producing covers for *Vanity Fair* among other projects

1930

Bauhaus moves to Berlin under Mies van der Rohe. Eric Gill's *Typography* is published

1933

Bauhaus closes. Tschichold arrested by Nazis. Henry Beck's *London Underground* Map

1934

Herbert Matter's Swiss travel posters

2.3

Art Deco and American Modernism

1918

E. McNight Kauffer produces *Daily Herald* poster

1924

Erté commissioned by *Harpers Bazaar*

1925

Exposition Internationale des Arts Decoratifs et Industriels Modernes in Paris. A. M. Cassandre's poster for *l'Intransigeant* newspaper

1939

New York's World Fair, for which Joseph Binder designs promotional posters. World War II breaks out

2.1

Early Modernism and Avant-garde Experimentation

The advent of World War I and the continuing growth in importance of the machine marked a change in the practice of graphic design. This period saw design become a part of a climate of experimentation in art. A number of movements reassessed how word and image were used to communicate. Futurism, Dadaism, Constructivism and De Stijl all developed new ways of thinking about visual and verbal representation that were to have far-reaching effects for graphic design.

Visual Elements

_ Questioned traditional forms of representation

_ Redefined the relationship between the spoken and the written word

_ Unconventional, non-linear and expressive layout of text

_ Use of abstracted imagery, found imagery and objects

_ Use of primary colours with neutral black, white and grey

_ Collage and photomontage

Right **Hugo Ball, 'Karawane', page from unpublished anthology *Dadaco*, 1920** Dadaism was motivated by a reaction to the futility of war and conventional social and artistic values to produce work designed to shock. The movement adopted the name Dada at random, possibly from the French word for a child's hobby horse, thus characterizing the nonsensical nature of Dadaist work. Artists associated with Dada often employed a range of techniques to juxtapose image, text and found objects in unexpected ways. Ball's poem, combining nonsensical words together in typical Dadaist style, was written in 1916. The use of a variety of type styles emphasizes its meaningless quality.

Opposite **Fortunato Depero, *Depero Futurista* (also known as the bolted book), Italy, 1927** Prior to the war, Italian Futurism had seen type become an explosive force in a sort of picture poetry that expressed both the discordance and the excitement of the Machine Age. Futurists aimed to free words from both literary and typographic convention. Layouts abandoned the strict vertical and horizontal axes implied by the letterpress process in favour of dynamic compositions that related more closely to actual speech and sound.

Fortunato Depero applied Futurist principles to more mainstream work during the 1920s. His bolted book shows a collection of his experimental typographic and advertising work. Although a thousand copies of the book were published, only a few have the metal binding seen here. This questions the use of traditional materials and demonstrates the importance of the machine as an icon of the modern world in Futurist thought. Depero breaks up geometric letterforms here with the stark use of black and white to highlight the shapes produced when they overlap.

KARAWANE

jolifanto bambla ô falli bambla
grossiga m'pfa habla horem
égiga goramen
higo bloiko russula huju
hollaka hollala
anlogo bung
blago bung
blago bung
bosso fataka
ü üü ü
schampa wulla wussa
hej tatta gôrem
eschige zunbada
wulubu ssubudu uluw ssubudu
tumba ba- umf
kusagauma
ba - umf

Hugo Ball   dada-kasserolle 1916

(1917)
Hugo Ball

DINAMO-AZARI

DEPERO FVTVRISTA

EDIZIONE ITALIANA
DINAMO
AZARI MILANO
Via S. Orsola, 6 - Telefono 82320
NEW-YORK-PARIS
BERLIN

egatura dinamo creazione Azari

Right **Theo van Doesburg, *De Stijl*, Issue 12, magazine cover, 1925** The Dutch De Stijl movement became a highly influential force across Europe. Seeking harmony and equilibrium in art and society using a non representational approach, this movement understood horizontal and vertical lines and primary colours to be the fundamental elements that defined the world. Asymmetrical layouts often incorporated rectangular forms and unconventional typefaces. The design of its journal is indicative of its concerns: asymmetrical layouts often incorporate rectangular forms and unconventional typefaces. This cover for one of the later issues of *De Stijl*, which was edited and designed by Van Doesburg, replaces the original masthead with a simple sans serif type against a field of unadorned negative space.

Opposite **The Foundry, *Architype Van Doesburg*, 1993, typeface based on Theo van Doesburg's original of 1919** Theo van Doesburg's 1919 typeface was based on letters he had constructed using letterpress rules, and was itself designed using a geometric grid of squares. This was sensitively revived in a digital form as *Architype Van Doesburg* by Freda Sack and David Quay of The Foundry.

ABCDEFGHIJKLM
NOPQRSTUVWXYZ
0123456789

2.2

European Modernism and the New Typography

The 1920s and 1930s saw designers build on the experimentation of the previous decade. Techniques like photography, collage and photomontage were associated with a progressive modernity in design, as were nonfigurative representation and the dynamic visual and typographic compositions of the New Typography. Many of the pioneers of modern design attended or taught at the Bauhaus, a German design school that offered models for both modern graphic design and design education. Influenced by Russian Constructivism and the De Stijl movement, the graphic work produced at the school sought to create a visual idiom that was suitable for a new world and which had the capacity to be universally understood. The aim was to create design solutions that would communicate messages as efficiently as possible, presenting information clearly and objectively.

Visual Elements

_ Aimed to be objective, rational, universal, functional and efficient

_ Use of all upper- or all lower-case letters, and sans serif typefaces based on geometric forms

_ Asymmetrical grid-like layouts

_ Abstract imagery and pure geometric shapes

_ Primary colours, often one primary colour with black

_ Letterpress, photography and photomontage

Opposite **Jan Tschichold, *Konstructivisten*, poster, Switzerland, 1937** This poster shows a reductivist use of primary elements both to reflect the approach taken to the Constructivist works on exhibition and to create clarity. It uses the asymmetrical composition and balance of typographic and geometric elements advocated by Tschichold in his influential book *Die Neue Typographie* (1928). Tschichold is also known for his redesign of Penguin publications with the introduction of a systematic house style between 1946 and 1949. Ultimately he rejected the New Typography in favour of a traditional approach.

● vom 16. januar bis 14. februar 1937

kunsthalle basel

konstruktivisten

van doesburg
domela
eggeling
gabo
kandinsky
lissitzky
moholy-nagy
mondrian
pevsner
taeuber
vantongerloo
vordemberge
u. a.

Right **Herbert Matter, *Die Schweiz im Schnee*, publication, Switzerland, 1935** The design of this publication shows the application of Bauhaus thought in its approach to typography, layout and photomontage. Similar in style to Matter's designs for a series of posters commissioned by the Swiss National Tourist Office, this one uses contrasting scale, a diagonal placement of image and type, and overprinting of colour in a dynamic asymmetrical composition. Photomontage was used extensively in modernism, both in artistic avant-garde experiments and in commercial design. The technique of juxtaposing such imagery in unexpected ways was clearly divorced from more traditional artistic production, which was associated with the old guard both artistically and socially. Matter later moved to New York, where he produced work for *Vogue*, *Harper's Bazaar*, the Container Corporation of America and Knoll.

Opposite **Bauer's *Futura*, typeface based on Paul Renner's original of 1928** The modernist approach to typeface design was to rationalize letterforms, reflecting the wider concern with form that followed function. The favoured typefaces were sans serif, which did away with outdated or unnecessary ornament and were based instead on pure geometric shapes. Herbert Bayer's *Universal*, Rudolf Koch's *Kabel* and Paul Renner's *Futura* all reflect these concerns. Renner designed *Futura* for the Bauer Type Foundry in Germany. He believed that designers should begin to look beyond tradition and respond to the needs of their own times. *Futura* became one of the most widely used typefaces in this period.

abcdefghijklmnopqr
stuvwxyzABCDEFGH
IJKLMNOPQRSTUVW
XYZ 0123456789

Qq

Right **Piet Zwart, spread from *NKF, NV Nederlandsche Kabelfabriek* (catalogue for the Dutch Cable Factory), the Netherlands, 1928** This catalogue shows the application of the New Typography in a commercial context. The dynamic layouts echo the combination of panoramic shots, photomontage, and tilted and zooming camera angles seen in Russian films of the period. Zwart employed the technique of photomontage, using close-up and cross-section shots of the cables alongside bold sans serif headlines and geometric shapes. He continued the cinematic feeling of the individual spreads throughout the catalogue by alternating vertical or horizontal and diagonal layouts. The primary colours in this spread are used in conjunction with the technique of overprinting; a blue half-tone was printed over red, leaving a blue image on white but a purple image on red. Zwart's approach is reflected in his description of himself as a '*typotekt*', an architect of type.

Opposite **Otto Neurath and Gerd Arntz, spread from *Modern Man in the Making*, the Netherlands, 1940** We are accustomed to seeing pictograms used for information graphics, but this system of communication was first developed in a modern way by Otto Neurath, a Viennese sociologist, between the 1920s and the 1940s. This example shows how he aimed to make complex quantitative information accessible to a universal audience by grouping and colour-coding symbols, a visual language known as Isotype. Gerd Arntz created the original symbols in linocut, and they were later reproduced using type-high letterpress lineblocks.

World Imperia

A.D.

Imperium Romanum   China

800

Arabian Empire

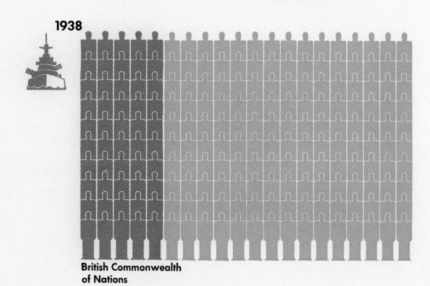

1250

Mongolian Empire

1938

British Commonwealth
of Nations

Each man symbol represents 10 million population

ISOTYPE

2.3

Art Deco and American Modernism

The inter-war years also saw the emergence of Art Deco, a decorative and luxurious style often associated with sophistication and the vibrancy of the Jazz Age. It favoured streamlined and geometric forms inspired by speed and the machine, as well as approaches inspired by the contemporary interest in ancient Egyptian and other cultures. Packaging and promotional work in the Art Deco style added modern appeal to a range of commercial products. Dynamic, simplified forms in flat colours were combined with typefaces that managed to be both modern and ornamental at the same.

Visual Elements

_ Decorative and luxurious

_ Abstract imagery

_ Geometric shapes and patterns

_ Use of motifs based on industrial forms, on speed or travel and on ancient Egyptian art

_ Simplified sans serif typefaces based on geometric forms

_ Vibrant colour combinations, and large blocks of solid and graduated colour

Right **Eau de Cologne aux Fleurs, label, France, early 20th century** Packaging and promotional work in the Art Deco style added modern appeal to a range of commercial products. Dynamic, simplified forms in flat colours were combined with typefaces that managed to be both modern and ornamental at the same time.

Opposite top **Linotype's *Bifur*, typeface based on A. M. Cassandre's original of 1929** Cassandre designed several typefaces for the Deberny et Peignot type foundry in France. Despite their simplicity, his designs for *Bifur* (1929), *Acier Noir* (1936) and *Peignot* (1937) provided an alternative to the functional typefaces of more avant-garde European modernism. *Bifur* was intended as a display type, each letter combining strong geometric elements with a pattern of lines, forcing the eye to fill in the missing sections. Characteristic of Cassandre's illustrative work are his use of bold two-dimensional forms and blocks of colour.

Opposite centre **P22 Font Foundry (by Dave Farey and Richard Dawson), *Johnston*, 1999, typeface based on Edward Johnson's alphabet for the London Underground, 1916** Johnston's original alphabet was conceived as a display face that would bring clarity and consistency to company signage. He made horizontals and verticals the same thickness, and based rounded letterforms on perfect circles. The original face was used until the 1980s. Farey and Dawson's 1999 revival was based on careful research of both the original alphabet and its designer, and aimed to render the font usable for text as well as display purposes.

Opposite below **Linotype's *Broadway*, typeface based on Morris Fuller Benton's original of 1928** Benton's design for the display face *Broadway* followed the Art Deco fashion for stylized, geometric and sophisticated letterforms. Lowercase and engraved versions were created by Sol Hess for Lanston Monotype in 1928.

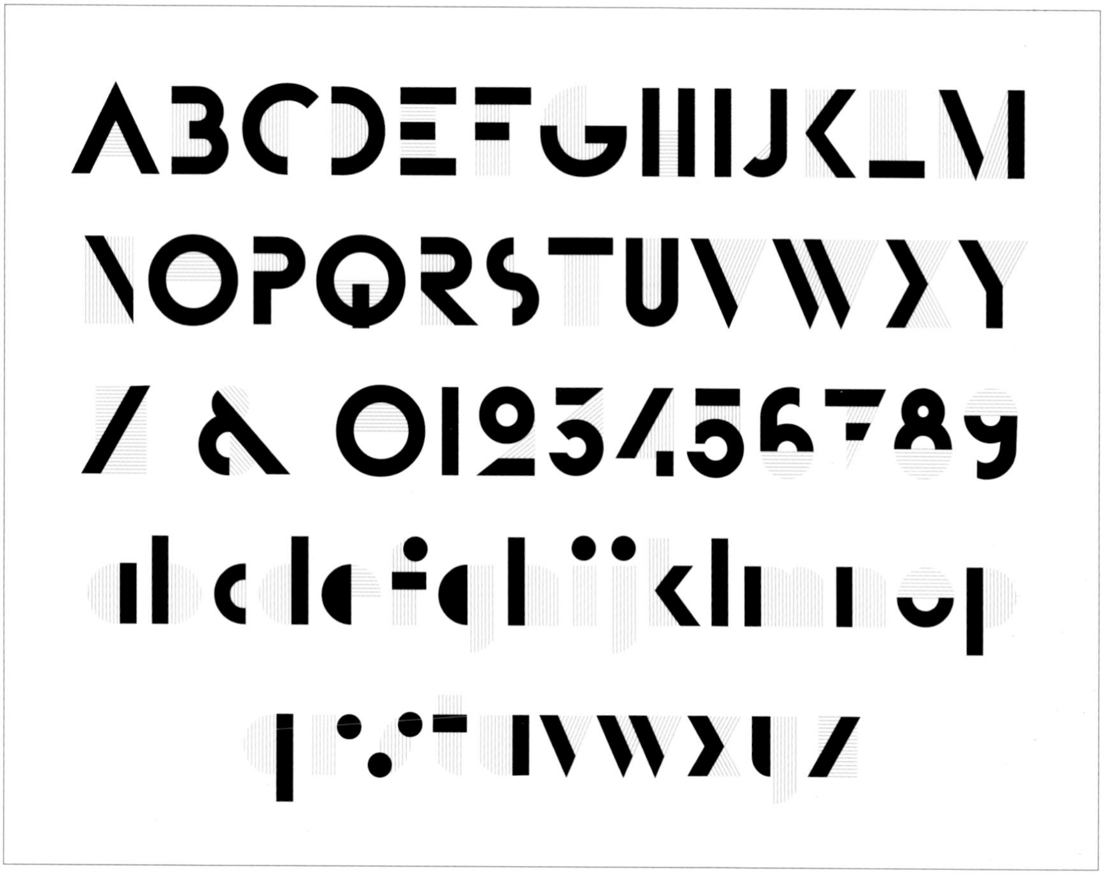

ABCDEFGHIJKLM
NOPQRSTUVWXY
Z & 0123456789
abcdefghijklmnop
qrstuvwxyz

Bb abcdefghijklmnopqrstuvwxyz
ABCDEFGHIJKLMNOPQRSTUV
WXYZ 0123456789

Qq abcdefghijklmnopqrstuvwxyz
ABCDEFGHIJKLMNOPQRSTUV
XYZ 0123456789

Right **Eduardo Garcia Benito, cover of** *Vogue***, US, 15 June 1927** The American version of *Vogue* first appeared in the 1890s but really only came to prominence after 1909, when it was bought by Condé Nast. Its covers give a real sense of the sophistication of the Jazz Age, frequently showing modern young women engaged in a range of social and sporting activities in elegant poses. This was a new type of magazine cover showing both a model and a title, in which the masthead changed according to the illustration. Eduardo Garcia Benito's design for this cover shows a mannequin-style head sporting a geometrically patterned swimming hat and incorporating the title in a beach ball. The use of dynamic colour combinations often emphasized the geometric patterns of Art Deco, evoking the flamboyance of the era.

Opposite top left and right **Alvin Lustig,** *Euclid***, typeface, US, 1939** Lustig only designed these few letters for the typeface *Euclid*. The accompanying sheet of letterpress printed geometric shapes on the right is one he used at that time to create letterforms. His widow, Elaine Lustig-Cohen, designed a new alphabet called *Euclid* in 2005, dedicating it to Alvin.

Opposite centre **P22 Font Foundry,** *Art Deco Chic***, typeface, US** Based on original streamlined forms, this elegant typeface was designed by P22 as part of their Art Deco Set, and echoes the refined hand-drawn letters of Eduardo Garcia Benito's cover for *Vogue*.

Opposite below **Linotype's** *Stencil***, typeface based on Gerry Powell's original of 1938** Powell looked to the utilitarian signage used for crates or other vernacular items to create *Stencil* for American Type Founders. Designed on the eve of World War II, it recalls military and other everyday forms of communication of the period.

SUMMER TRAVEL NUMBER

JUNE 15 · 1927   © The Condé Nast Publications *Inc.*   PRICE 35 CENTS

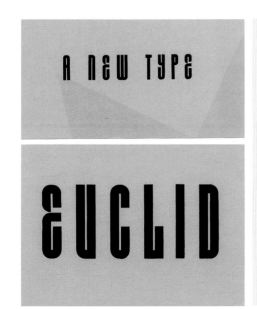

A NEW TYPE

EUCLID

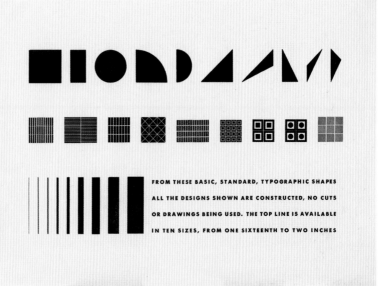

FROM THESE BASIC, STANDARD, TYPOGRAPHIC SHAPES ALL THE DESIGNS SHOWN ARE CONSTRUCTED, NO CUTS OR DRAWINGS BEING USED. THE TOP LINE IS AVAILABLE IN TEN SIZES, FROM ONE SIXTEENTH TO TWO INCHES

abcdefghijklmnopqrstuvwxyz
ABCDEFGHIJKLMNOPQRSTUVWXYZ
1234567890

ABCDEFGHIJKLMNOPQRS
TUVWXYZ 0123456789

1945–1965 Mid-century Modern

3.1
The International Style

1918
Ernst Keller joins the Zurich Kunstgewerbeschule

1927
Max Bill studies at the Bauhaus

1931
Max Bill adopts the concepts laid down by Theo van Doesburg in his *Manifesto of Art Concret* (1930)

1939
Herman Zapf begins work at Koch's printing firm in Frankfurt

1947
Emil Ruder and Armin Hoffman begin teaching at the Allegemeine Gewerbeschule in Basel

1949
Carlo L. Vivarelli's *Für das Alter* poster

1950
The Hochschule für Gestaltung in Ulm is planned. Siegfried Odermatt opens design studio in Zurich. Zapf's *Palatino* typeface is released

1952
Rudolph de Harak opens studio in New York

1954
Adrian Frutiger produces *Univers* typeface. Zapf's book *Typographicum* is first published

1936
Giovanni Pintori joins the Olivetti Corporation

1937
Paul Rand begins work as an editorial and promotional designer

1939
Bradbury Thompson begins designing *Westvaco Inspirations,* a promotional publication for printing papers

1940
Alex Steinweiss becomes art director of Columbia Records. First edition of *Print* magazine. Abram Games designs posters for the War Office in Britain

1942
Cipe Pineles is made art director of *Glamour* magazine

1945
Alvin Lustig designs book covers for New Directions. George Olden joins Columbia Broadcasting System (CBS) as designer

1946
Rand's *Thoughts on Design* is published. Lou Dorfsman becomes art director at CBS radio

1947
Pintori designs logotype for Olivetti. Jan Tschichold begins work for Penguin Books

1948
F.H.K. Henrion establishes Studio H, later Henrion Design Associates, in Britain

1949
Doyle Dane Bernbach advertising agency is established. Leo Lionni becomes art director of *Fortune* magazine

1960
Saul Bass designs graphics for the film *Exodus.* Helmut Krone's Volkswagen campaign for Doyle Dane Bernbach

1962
Peter Palazzo becomes design editor of the *New York Herald Tribune*

1963
International Council of Graphic Design Associations (ICOGRADA) is established

1964
Lou Dorfsman becomes director of design for whole CBS corporation. Chermayeff and Geismar Associates design Mobil Oil trademark. CCA establish the Centre for Advanced Research in Design in US. Minale Tattersfield established in London

1968
F.H.K. Henrion publishes *Design Coordination and Corporate Image*

1957	1958	1959	1960	1961	1965	1967	1968	1972	**3.2**
Anthony Froshaug joins Ulm's teaching staff and sets up the typography workshop	Zapf's *Optima* typeface is released	The journal *New Graphic Design*, founded by Josef Müller-Brockmann, Hans Neuburg, Richard P. Lohse and Carlo Vivarelli, begins publication	Müller-Brockmann's *Weniger Larm* poster. Rudolph de Harak's series of book covers for McGraw-Hill Publishers	*Neue Haas Grotesk* typeface is renamed *Helvetica* on its release in Germany	Armin Hofmann's *Graphic Design Manual is* published	Ruder's *Typography: A Manual of Design* is published. Jacqueline S. Casey's *Ocean Engineering* poster for MIT's Design Services Office in US	Anton Stankowski commissioned to produce design programme for Berlin. Ulm school of design closes	Ralph Coburn's poster for the *MIT Jazz Band* for the Design Services Office	**The New York Style; Corporate Identity; Post-war Optimism and Populuxe**

1951	1952	1953	1955	1956	1957	1959
William Golden made creative director at CBS and designs their logotype. Dorfsman and Andy Warhol produce *Living off the Main Line* advertisement for CBS. James K. Fogleman hired as design director of CIBA Pharmaceutical Products. Games designs logo for the Festival of Britain. Blue Note Records founder Alfred Lion, photographer Francis Wolff and Reid Miles emphasize the design of their covers	Saul Bass opens own design studio. Games designs British Broadcasting Corporation (BBC) logo	Otto Storch named art director of *McCall's* magazine. Henry Wolf becomes art director of *Esquire* magazine. Allen Hurlburt joins *Look* magazine as art director. Gene Federico's advertisement for *Women's Day* in *New Yorker* magazine. CIBA Pharmaceutical Products Incorporated in New Jersey initiates corporate-identity programme	Bass designs film titles and promotional material for Otto Preminger's *The Man with the Golden Arm*. Leo Lionni's promotional material for 'The Family of Man' exhibition at MOMA, New York	Pintori's *Elettrosumma 22* poster for Olivetti. Rand produces IBM trademark. Herbert Matter produces brochures for Knoll. Games made art director for Pengiun.	Brownjohn, Chermayeff and Geismar design office established. Chermayeff's cover for the Boston Symphony album *Eroica*. William Golden and Ben Shahn produce *The Big Push* advertisement for CBS. Ralph Eckerstrom produces trademark for Container Corporation of America	*Communication Arts* begins publication. Robert Miles Runyan produces *Litton Industries Annual Report*. Lionni produces the children's book *Little Blue and Yellow*. Henrion designs corporate identity for KLM

53

3.1

The International Style

This period produced some of the most memorable and abiding graphic design of the last century: the fields of advertising, corporate identity and editorial design emerged as arenas for innovative work that was concept-driven. Emerging in the 1950s, the International Style, or Swiss School, inherited its approach from the modernism of the preceding decades. Focusing on finding a solution specific to the content of a given brief, designers emphasized the clear and objective organization of information. The movement became truly universal, spreading from Europe to America, and has remained an influential force to this day.

Visual Elements

_ Motivated by objectivity and clarity in the presentation of information

_ Adherence to a typographic grid with emphasis on a vertical / horizontal axis

_ Sans serif typefaces such as *Akzidenz Grotesk*, *Univers* and *Helvetica*

_ Large headlines running horizontally, vertically or diagonally

_ Narrow columns of body text, ranged to the left

_ Photographic or geometric, technical imagery

Right **Linotype's *Univers*, based on Adrian Frutiger's 1954 original** Adrian Frutiger's *Univers* has achieved 'classic' status. Designed for the Paris firm of Deberny et Peignot, *Univers* has a slight calligraphic quality when compared to the more geometrically constructed typefaces of the modern movement. Frutiger's rationalist approach to the design of the typeface extended to his use of numbers to identify the variety of widths and weights rather than the more traditional terms. *Univers 55* is a regular weight, making *Univers 39* light and extra condensed and *Univers 83* expanded and extra bold.
Opposite **Armin Hofmann, *Giselle,* poster, Municiple Theatre, Basel, Switzerland, 1959** Posters of the International Movement are characterized by the careful juxtaposition of cropped photographic or abstract imagery and lettering to produce dynamic compositions. This approach stems from the rationality and objectivity at the heart of post-war Swiss design.

From 1955–1968, Armin Hofmann was commissioned to design the poster campaigns for the Municipal Theatre in Basel. In this fine example for the ballet *Giselle*, the vertical placement of the main text turns the headline into an abstract visual element in its own right. The precise placement of the dot on the 'i' is a central element in this beautifully balanced interaction between visual components. The circular dot replaces the more conventional square form. Hofmann designed and cut out the lettering for the title by hand, a feature that is characteristic of much of his work. *Akzidenz Grotesk* was then used for the smaller text in the top left corner of the poster, rather than the more rectilinear *Helvetica* or *Univers* fonts.

abcdefghijklmn
opqrstuvwxyz
ABCDEFGHIJKLMN
OPQRSTUVWXYZ
0123456789

Bb

Right **Sainsbury's packaging, UK, early 1960s**
During the 1960s supermarket chains introduced own-label goods. Developed by their in-house studio under Peter Dixon, Sainsbury's simple, consistent approach to packaging lent their brand an air of confident modernity, standing in contrast to the attention-grabbing designs of other manufacturers. Their reliance on type rather than image, the use of a clear grid-like layout and the restrained use of colour demonstrate the impact of the International Style on the high street.

Below right **Linotype's *Helvetica*, typeface based on Edouard Hoffmann and Max Miedinger's original of 1957** Initially, designers of the International Movement favoured the use of *Akzidenz Grotesk*, a 19th-century typeface. However, the contemporary typefaces *Univers* and *Helvetica* also became popular. Designed by Edouard Hoffmann and Max Miedinger, *Helvetica*'s letterforms were embraced for their ability to make an impact through the interplay of negative and positive space. *Helvetica* was first released as *Neue Haas Grotesk* by the Haas Type Foundry in 1957 and as *Helvetica* (the Latin name for Switzerland) by the Stempel foundry in 1961. A digital version, Linotype's *Neue Helvetica*, was released in 1983.

Opposite **Book covers for Penguin UK: Germano Facetti, *Dreadful Summit*, by Stanley Ellin, 1964 and *Busman's Honeymoon,* by Dorothy L. Sayers, 1963; and Romek Marber, *The Second Curtain,* by Roy Fuller, 1962, and *No Love Lost*, by Margery Allingham, 1961** These and other Penguin covers have become widely associated with the periods in which they were designed, and offer a sort of shorthand for the look of the era. Using a grid designed by Romek Marber under the art directorship of Germano Facetti, their design created both clarity and impact on the shelf. Colour, type, layout and imagery were all used to unify the series. The colour green, already associated with Penguin's crime titles, was retained while a layout that separated out the publisher's and series names from the title and author of the book with narrow rules allowed the consumer to distinguish information easily. Marber used *Intertype Standard*, a version of *Akzidenz Grotesk* which had first been designed at the Berthold Foundry at the turn of the century and was subsequently revived by practitioners of the International Style. Like other titles in the series, the images used by Marber and Facetti here suggest the content of the novels without illustrating it in a literal way. The two-colour process was extended by the use of overprinting and reversing out, characteristic techniques of this period. A third colour was sometimes used, as in Facetti's design for *Dreadful Summit*.

abcdefghijklmn
opqrstuvwxyz
ABCDEFGHIJKLMN
OPQRSTUVWXYZ
0123456789

Gg

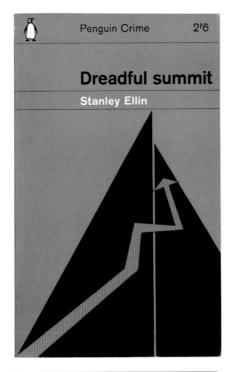

Penguin Crime   2'6

Dreadful summit

Stanley Ellin

Penguin Crime   5/-

Busman's honeymoon

Dorothy L. Sayers

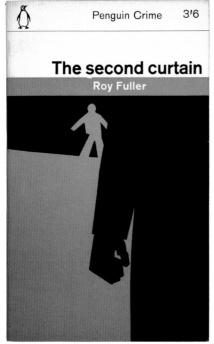

Penguin Crime   3'6

The second curtain

Roy Fuller

Penguin Crime   2'6

No love lost

Margery Allingham

3.2

The New York Style; Corporate Identity

The New York Style emerged in the mid-20th century as a particularly American approach to graphic design. Although rooted in modernism, it is often defined by its attention to concept and by its use of wit and humour. Designers considered images and typography as a whole to communicate symbolically and with immediacy. The fields of editorial, corporate and advertising design developed apace during this period, providing a forum for this innovative and powerful approach to visual communication.

Visual Elements

_ Concept-driven approach often employing humour and wit in a variety of styles

_ Playful and integrated use of type and image

_ Contrasts in colour and scale

_ Use of traditional, solid typefaces like *Bodoni* alongside simple sans serifs and script faces

_ Collage, cutout-style illustration

_ Colour photography with high saturation value

Right **Ivan Chermayeff, cover of *The Wisdom of the Heart* by Henry Miller, US, 1959** The conceptual approach is seen in Chermayeff's cover for *The Wisdom of the Heart*. A black rather than the expected red heart is used as a substitute head, underlining the connection between the 'wisdom' and 'heart' of the title.

Opposite top left **Saul Bass, *8th San Francisco International Film Festival*, poster, US, 1964** Saul Bass's poster encapsulates its subject in a concept linking national identity and film in an image of film strips as national flags, symbols or colours. Bass is best known for his clever promotional title work for film using collage cutouts, drawn letterforms and bright colours.

Opposite top right **Doyle Dane Bernbach, 'Think Small', advertisement for Volkswagen, US, 1960** A new style of advertisement moved away from the crowded examples that consumers had been used to towards a dynamic use of space, typography and photographic imagery. This approach emerged from the joint development of concepts between copywriters and designers, and called on audiences to make their own connections between text and image in the communication of the 'big idea'. Doyle Dane Bernbach's groundbreaking campaign for Volkswagen turned possible 'flaws' in the product into benefits. Here, the scale of the image and white space were used to develop the concept, while the *Futura Semi Bold* typeface adds a rational, Germanic edge. The concept's strength becomes more obvious when one considers that automobile adverts during this period frequently focused on size, elaborate styling and associations with affluence and luxury.

Opposite below **Bauer Bodoni, typeface based on Heinrich Jost and Louis Hoell's original of 1926** Immensely popular in the 1950s, *Bauer Bodoni* was originally designed by Heinrich Jost and cut by Louis Hoell for the Bauer Type Foundry in Germany in 1926. It was closely based on the late 18th-century fonts of Giambattista Bodoni, characterized by a contrast between bold stems and elegant hairlines.

The Wisdom of the Heart by Henry Miller
a new directions paperbook

Right **Michael Doret, *Metroscript*, typeface for
Alphabet Soup, US, 2007–8** Type designer Michael
Doret states that the design for *Metroscript* is an
amalgamation of a number of different popular hand-
lettered styles from the 1920s to the 1950s. This style
of lettering also became known in the US as a 'baseball'
or 'sports script' (see page 185).

Opposite left **Alvin Lustig, jacket of *The Wanderer*
by Alain Fournier, US, 1946** Lustig's jacket designs
evolved from a distillation of his thoughts on reading the
books in question. Moving away from the compositor's
tray towards his own mark-making, his designs for the
publisher New Directions were influenced by the work
of the European painters Miró, Klee and Matisse, and
engaged readers by demanding their reflection. The
subdued use of colour here is evocative of the 1940s.

Opposite right **Alvin Lustig, 'Economy' and 'Form',
advertisements for Knoll, US, *c.* 1945** The influence
of European modernism underpins much American work
of the 1940s and 1950s. Lustig's advertisements for
Knoll embody the abstract, reductivist approach to form
associated with the company's furniture design, and
indeed with the progressive modernism of the
company's image.

economy

through mass-production and standardization, our furniture provides economic, flexible usefulness for home...housing...and institution.

H. G. KNOLL associates 601 MADISON AVENUE, NEW YORK 22, NEW YORK

form

Clarity of form is a basic element of good contemporary furniture. This rocker, designed by Ralph Rapson, exemplifies the honest design characteristic of all H. G. Knoll products.

H. G. KNOLL associates 601 MADISON AVENUE, NEW YORK 22, NEW YORK

Below **Paul Rand, Westinghouse logo, US, 1960,
and IBM logo, US, 1956; and Ivan Chermayeff
and Tom Geismar, Mobil Oil logo, US, 1964,
and Chase Manhattan Bank logo, US, 1963**
The broadening of market boundaries and the growth
of consumer society that followed World War II
prompted the further development of design for corporate
identity. This period produced some of the most
longstanding identities of the corporate world. Rand's
work for IBM and Westinghouse and Chermayeff and
Geismar's work for Chase Manhattan Bank and Mobil
Oil continue to be highly visible.

Opposite **Giovanni Pintori, *Olivetti Lexikon*, poster,
Italy, 1953** Olivetti was an early proponent of corporate
identity, applying a consistent style to their products,
architecture and promotional pieces. Giovanni Pintori
worked with the firm from the 1930s, producing
memorable high-quality work, including the logotype
and the advertisement shown here. This was one of
a series of posters in which he used a combination of
bright colour, illustration or collage and photographs to
depict the function of the product as well as the product
itself. Here, colour and image suggest the movement
of typewriter keys.

3.2

Post-war Optimism and Populuxe

It is perhaps the popular graphics of the 1940s and 1950s that are most widely evocative of this period. Often produced by printers rather than designers, adverts, menus, signs and packaging frequently show combinations of script-like typefaces and playful stock images. During the 1940s, colour in print often had a dusty quality, and the impression was of chalky, muted colours. The period following World War II saw colour magazines and Hollywood films both create and respond to consumer expectation: the increased use of saturated, scarcely real and sometimes off-register colour in postcards and advertisements frames our own vision of post-war optimism.

Visual Elements

_ Inspired by post-war optimism, belief in the future and the growth of a consumer society

_ Combinations of blocky san serif lettering, revivals of sturdy 19th-century display types, and script typefaces

_ Space-age, futuristic, biomorphic and scientifically inspired imagery and motifs

_ Stock art images showing everything from cartoon-like characters to smartly dressed and affluent figures

_ Collage-style imagery

_ Eye-catching primaries and bright pastel colours

Top right **Cadbury's _Lucky Numbers_, biscuit tin, UK, 1950s** The collage-style design, combination of numerical and lettering styles, and pastel colouring are typical of packaging at this time. The use of 19th-century type styles for some of the numbers indicates how the Festival of Britain made its presence felt in everyday life. The impact of space-age technology and scientific discovery was also visible in all fields of design, whether in the actual shapes of domestic products, in comic-book illustration or in the use of futuristic imagery on consumer goods. The lettering on the Lucky Numbers tin shows the influence of science in its imitation of recently discovered molecular structures.

Below right **Linotype's _Chisel_, typeface based on Robert Harling's original of 1939** _Chisel_ recalls engraved Latin letterforms. Harling also designed _Playbill_, a typeface based on 19th-century display fonts.

Opposite top left **Abram Games, Festival of Britain catalogue, UK, 1951** Although we might not consider this beautifully designed symbol as Populuxe, the Festival of Britain did express the mood of post-war morale boosting. Abram Games managed to combine a sense of modernity and tradition in his designs for the event's visual identity: his 'emblem' adopts a modernist style while type from the previous century surrounds it. The festival's typographic panel advocated the use of 19th-century faces to create a sense of Britishness and forge a visual link with the Great Exhibition of 1851.

Opposite top right **Festival of Britain bus tickets for London Transport, UK, 1951** London Transport issued a series of tickets for eight special bus services that linked some Festival sights together and made others more accessible. The use of bright colours and imagery gave these tickets an air of celebration, while the texture of ink and paper and the slightly off-register quality of the printing reflect the throwaway nature of such ephemera.

Opposite below **Monotype's _Festival Titling_, typeface based on Philip Boydell's original of 1950** Cut by Monotype, this typeface was designed as the official face of the Festival of Britain. It became more generally available in 1952. Like _Chisel_, it echoes the three dimensions of engraved letterforms but in a sans serif face.

64

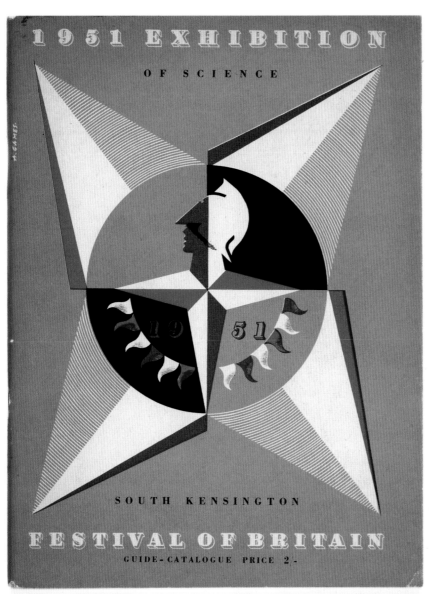

AB ABCDEFGHIJKLMNOPQR STUVWXYZ 0123456789

Left **Advertisements and promotional pieces, 1957–58** These adverts demonstrate how vernacular ephemera frequently employed combinations of script typefaces and stock imagery. Cartoon figures often both created movement and added humour. The advertisement for Fortnum & Mason (far left), perhaps produced using the technique of linocut, demonstrates great skill in pattern-making. Seasonal catalogues for the shop that the artist Edward Bawden created for the advertising agency Colman, Prentice and Varley between 1955 and 1958 show the same strong line, technique and use of animal motifs. Bawden also produced designs for Walker's Warrington Ales, Gilbey's Gin, Irish Air Lines, London Transport and Imperial Airways, among others.

Opposite top left **'Bring Home a Broadway Show!', advertisement for Decca Records in the** *Evening Post*, **UK, 1946** This advert seems to both respond to competition from the cinema and pre-empt the impact that television was to have in the following decade, promising all the glamour of show business in the comfort and accessibility of the home. Advertisements like this one sold everything from cars to refrigerators, promising an affluent lifestyle and domestic bliss to a new generation of homemakers. Archetypal figures like the well-dressed young man shown here reflected the belief that the American dream was available to all. Colour photography, now more easily reproduced with photolithography, as well as colour illustrations that imitated it were intended to impress consumers with their super-real quality.

Opposite top right **Surf soap-powder packaging for Lever Brothers, UK, 1952** Pre-war research into synthetic detergents came to fruition in the late 1940s, when shortages of ingredients for the manufacture of soap made their development a necessity. Surf was first manufactured in 1952, its packaging attracting consumer attention with the brand name shown in a strong script with a drop shadow, bright colours and copy, all of which promises to bring modernity itself into the home. By the 1960s, such products had to compete with one another on the new supermarket shelves.

Opposite below **Linotype's** *Cascade Script*, **typeface based on Matthew Carter's original of 1965** Known for his calligraphic script typefaces, Matthew Carter designed *Cascade* for Mergenthaler using new phototypesetting technology. Although designed in the 1960s, it evokes the script faces popular for ephemera in the 1940s.

Bring home a Broadway Show!

Big Broadway shows were only for the fortunate few. Tradition had always said so.

But Decca said No!

Believing that the best is none too good for *all* Americans, Decca put Broadway's best on records. Much of the magic of these plays came from the players' personalities. So Decca smashed tradition to record the original casts!

And soon dozens of glamorous hit shows took to the road on Decca records …with strictly Number One companies. Traveled to your town…into your home. Played their brilliant best for you and your family . . . for *millions* of families.

Decca's famous Original Cast Albums fulfill one part of Decca's promise to you. Decca will continue to bring you the good things you want to hear, recorded the way you want to hear them.

DECCA RECORDS

ANNIE GET YOUR GUN. Ethel Merman in new Irving Berlin musical. 12 sides. 10 inch. No. A-468. $5.25

CALL ME MISTER. Fresh, new revue of reconversion to civilian life. 10 sides. 10 inch. No. A-466. $4.50

OKLAHOMA! Fourth year on Broadway. Still America's favorite album. 12 sides. 10 inch. No. DA-359.....$5.25

CAROUSEL. Critics' Circle award for musical comedy. 10 sides. 12 inch. No. DA-400. $5.85

PORGY AND BESS. Gershwin's glorious folk opera. Rich in Americana. 8 sides. 12 inch. No. A-145.......$4.85

Prices do not include Federal, state or local taxes.

All with members of original New York casts.

Bb abcdefghijklmnopqrstuvwxyz
ABCDEFGHIJKLMNOPQRSTUVWXYZ
0123456789

1954–1980 Experimentation and Rationality

4.1	1954	1956	1957	1958	1959	1960	1961	1962
Counter-culture and Experimentation	Pushpin Studio established by Milton Glaser, Seymour Chwast, Reynolds Ruffins and Edward Sorel	'This Is Tomorrow' exhibition at the Whitechapel Art Gallery in London	Mary Quant's Bazaar clothing shop opens in London	Gerald Holton designs the Campaign for Nuclear Disarmament (CND) symbol	Fidel Castro defeats regime of President Fulgencio Batista in Cuba. German periodical *Twen* launched by Willy Fleekhaus	Art Nouveau exhibition at Museum of Modern Art, New York. Photo-typesetting becomes prevalent during this era	Castro dictates terms under which art and design can be produced – design and other popular art forms to be given emphasis over the fine arts. Later the Cuban Commission for Revolutionary Action is established with Félix Beltrán as art director, and the Organisation for Solidarity with the People of Africa, Asia and Latin America distributes posters abroad	Cuban Missile Crisis. Roman Cieslewicz's *Cyrk* poster. Franciszek Starowiejski's *Warsaw Drama Theatre* poster

1970	1974	1975	1976	1979	1980	**4.2**	1952	1954
Barry Zaid's cover design for Bevis Hillier's *Art Deco*. Peter Max's 'Love' graphic. Robert Massin's *Letter and Image* is published. Pierre Bernard, François Miehe and Gerard Paris-Clavel form the French design studio Grapus. Peter Brandt's anti-Vietnam War poster *Q: And Babies? A: And Babies*. Jamie Reid founds *The Suburban Press*, a radical community newspaper, in Britain	Waldemar Swierzy's *Jimi Hendrix* poster	Vietnam War ends	Jamie Reid works full time for the Sex Pistols	Sandanistas defeat the Somoza dictatorship in Nicaragua – the Sandanista government later founds a national art school	Jerzy Janiszewski's *Solidaranosc* logo	Humour and Rationality	Herbert Spencer's influential *Design in Business Printing* is published	Pieter Brattinga curates exhibitions at a gallery attached to De Jong and Co. printing works in Hilversum; he goes on to design the company's journal *Kwadraatblad*

1970	1975	1976	1977	1978	1979	1981	1983	1984	1985
Both Igarashi and Koichi Sato establish their own studios in Japan. Wim Crouwel and others establish Total Design in the Netherlands	Shigeo Fukuda designs his award-winning *Victory 1945* poster. Eiko Ishioka designs campaigns for Shiseido cosmetics	R.D.E Oxenaar appointed aesthetic adviser to the Netherlands Postal and Telecommuni-cations service	Gert Dumbar establishes Studio Dumbar in The Hague after studying in London's RCA. Holland's Frank Beekers, Lies Ros and Rob Schroder form Wild Plakken	The Dutch journal *Hard Werken* is launched by Henk Elenga, Gerard Hadders, Tom van der Haspel, Helen Howard, Rick Vermeulen and others. Later, Hard Werken Design studio is established. Japanese Graphic Designers Association replaces Japanese Advertising Artists Club	Anton Beeke's poster for the play *Leonce and Lena*	Ikko Tanaka's *Nihon Buyo* poster for UCLA's Asian Performing Arts Institute. Gert Dumbar commissioned to produce a visual identity for the Dutch Postal, Telegraph and Telephone Authority (PTT)	Igarashi begins designing his annual poster calendar for MOMA in New York and then for the Alphabet Gallery in Tokyo	Exhibition of Japanese design, 'Tradtion et Nouvelles' Techniques', in Paris – poster designed by Nagai	Igarashi's *Expo '85* poster

1963

Barbara Hulanicki opens Biba – John McConnell designs logo. *Oz* magazine is founded in London by Richard Neville. Bob Cato becomes head of creative services at CBS Records

1964

Vietnam War begins. Herbert Marcuse's *One-Dimensional Man* is published. Warsaw International Poster Biennial. Glaser produces record cover *The Sound of Harlem* for the Jazz Archive Series. Robert Massin and Henry Cohen design Eugene Ionesco's *La Cantatrice chauve*. Alphonse Mucha exhibition in London

1965

Exhibition on Jugendstijl and Expressionism held at University of California. Chwast's Elektra Productions promotional piece announcing Elektra's relocation. New York's *East Village Other* begins publication

1966

Gunther Keiser's *Alabama Blues* poster. Robert Massin's design for *Delire à deux*. LSD made illegal in California. Aubrey Beardsley exhibition in London

1967

San Francisco's Summer of Love. Wes Wilson's *Byrds, Byrds, Byrds* and Victor Moscoso's *Miller's Blues Band* posters. Martin Sharp designs *Mr Tambourine Man* poster. Glaser designs *Bob Dylan* poster for inclusion with album. Ernesto (Che) Guevara shot. Marshall McLuhan's *The Medium Is the Massage* is published

1968

Martin Luther King is assassinated. Student revolts in Paris. Soviet Union invades Czechoslovakia. Marshall McLuhan's *War and Peace in the Global Village* is published. Chwast's *End Bad Breath* poster. *Day of the Heroic Guerilla* poster depicting the iconic image of Che Guevara. Mexico Olympics. *Sgt. Pepper's Lonely Hearts Club Band* album

1958

The Masuda Tadashi Design Institute is established in Japan

1960

Japan Design Centre is established. The 1960s see the emergence of the Dutch Provo youth movement and experimental art movements like the neo-Dada Fluxus

1961

Ryuichi Yamashiro's *Tree Planting Campaign* poster. Eiko Ishioka graduates from Tokyo National University of Fine Arts

1962

Alan Fletcher, Bob Gill and Colin Forbes form Gill, Fletcher and Forbes design studio in Britain – later, the studio becomes Pentagram. Garland and Associates established in Britain. Total Design established by Wim Crouwel, among others, in Holland

1963

Ikko Tanaka establishes Tanaka Design Studio. Wim Crouwel designs for the Stedelijk Museum in Amsterdam

1964

Olympics held in Japan – Yusaku Kamekura designs its identity and promotional material

1965

R.D.E Oxenaar is first commissioned to design Dutch paper currency

1968

Takenobu Igarashi graduates from Tama University – he later studies at the University of California. Tadanori Yokoo's poster for Sixth International Biennial Exhibition of Prints, held in Tokyo

1969

Herbert Spencer's *Pioneers of Modern Typography* is published. First Parco department store opens – Eiko Ishioka becomes art director

1989

PTT identity revised by Studio Dumbar

4.1

Counter-culture and Experimentation

The cultural, social and political events of the 1960s and 1970s were to frame the nature of graphic design produced during these decades. A culture of protest, revolt and revolution is integral to some of this period's most experimental work: design for music in particular saw a new generation of images produced to appeal to new forms of youth culture, and poster design was used to register the discord generated by student protests, the Vietnam War and the civil rights movement.

Visual Elements

_ Reflected the questioning spirit of the age

_ A return to the use of found imagery and illustration

_ A strong interest in stylistic revivals of the late 19th and early 20th centuries

_ Distorted lettering

_ Vibrating or bright colour combinations

Right **Wes Wilson, *Byrds, Byrds, Byrds*, poster, US, 1967** The term *psychedelia* initially referred to the graphic art produced for concerts of underground and progressive music on the West Coast of America but went on to include work produced in Britain and elsewhere. It was defined by its use of vibrating colour combinations and distorted lettering, appealing to a new generation reacting against the norms of mainstream society. Psychedelic posters used both drawn and found imagery which was transformed through the use of colour and pattern.

A rise of interest in alternatives to the objectivity of the International Style coincided with exhibitions of Art Nouveau like that at New York's Museum of Modern Art (1960) and a shift away from dependence on the horizontal / vertical formats of letterpress technology. Psychedelic posters gave Art Nouveau motifs an entirely new flavour with an approach to colour and form that was peculiarly Sixties. In this poster for The Byrds and Moby Grape, Wes Wilson used a peacock, a favourite Art Nouveau motif, set against a distorted typeface influenced by those of the Vienna Secession. Vibrating colour, imagery and type all had to be decoded by the audience.

Some poster artists focused on achieving maximum impact by combining complementary colours: red with blue or orange with green, for example. Victor Moscoso was influenced in this by his teacher Josef Albers, who had published his *Interaction of Color* in 1963: 'He had these exercises in his colour class that drove everyone crazy. One was how to make a colour look like two different ones …Your retina conflicts with what you see – it is a visual trick.' More generally, ideas about optical vibration associated with Op Art and the discordant colour combinations of Pop Art were both influential, as were the increased range of dyes that became available during the 1960s and the effects of hallucinatory drugs. Henri Michaux, a writer and artist, for example, described his experience of LSD as 'an amazing film which sometimes slows down, comes to rest and halts, enabling me to contemplate a coloured image, whose colours are indeed magnificent'.

Opposite left **Seymour Chwast, *The Sensational Houdini*, poster, US, 1973** Other designers of this generation were also forging a new path by breaking away from the objectivity of the modern movement. The search for alternative imagery and the revival of ornament saw both the return of illustration as a central element in design and the use of an eclectic range of historical and cultural sources. This promotional piece combines a clever pastiche of 19th-century letterpress posters with the flat areas of colour of a more contemporary style of illustration. The development of new techniques and technologies like Letraset and

photocomposition saw designers become able to manipulate type in new ways, while silkscreen-printed posters and developments in commercial printing saw an explosion of colour on the street.

Opposite right **Milton Glaser, *Dylan*, poster for Columbia Records, US, 1966** Glaser was commissioned by Columbia Records to produce this poster to accompany a compilation album of Bob Dylan's hits. The album cover featured a photograph by Roland Scherman showing Dylan in profile. Continuing this theme, creative director Bob Cato sought out Glaser to create an image because of the way he used silhouettes in his illustrative work. In response, Glaser created an image that became iconic of 1960s America and that demonstrates his synthesis of several different references. The influences of a self-portrait by Marcel Duchamp, of Islamic design and of turn-of-the-century posters are all evident here. Dylan's name is spelled out in Glaser's *Babyteeth* typeface, inspired by a barber-shop sign in Mexico City.

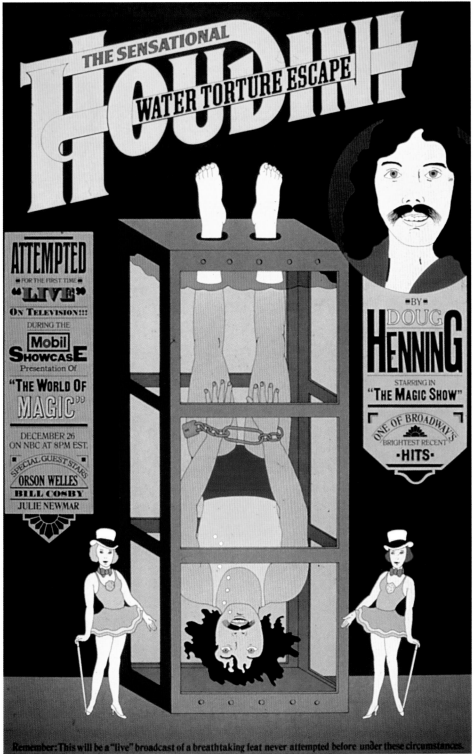

71

Right top and centre **Seymour Chwast, Artone logo, US, 1964, and** *Monograph* **typeface, US, 1972** Chwast and Glaser revived a range of typographic forms including those found on 19th-century letterpress posters, and in the Art Nouveau and Art Deco styles. *Monograph* shows Chwast's interest in what he termed 'Roxy' style, while his identity for Artone India ink both recalls Art Nouveau lettering and evokes a drop of ink or the curved form of the Artone bottle itself. The Artone identity became the basis for a complete display face, becoming tremendously popular following its inclusion in the Photo-Lettering, Inc. catalogue, despite Chwast's fears that the craze for Art Nouveau had already peaked.

Below right **John McConnell, Biba logo, UK, early 1960s** The mood of Swinging Sixties London is recalled for many by the styles of Mary Quant's Bazaar and Barbara Hulanicki's Biba boutiques. Rising incomes and social change saw the younger generation seeking to express their identities with an eclectic mix of affordable space-age and vintage styles. Various stylistic revivals in type, image and colour underpinned a wide range of work, lending products and events a young, anti-Establishment feel. The first Biba shop, opened in 1963, had an informal atmosphere with its Victorian furniture and objets d'art. McConnell's logo extended the vintage impression by using a Celtic knot treated in Art Nouveau style. The vogue for such stylistic resurrection was fed both by a general appetite for the novel and by more specific events like the exhibitions of the work of Alphonse Mucha (1963) and Aubrey Beardsley (1966) at London's Victoria & Albert Museum. The Art Deco style was made popular by a major exhibition in Paris in 1966 and by movies like *Bonnie and Clyde* (1967), *Thoroughly Modern Millie* (1967) and, later, *The Great Gatsby* (1974). A move to a former Art Deco-style department store in 1973 saw early Hollywood glamour become a more prominent aspect of Biba's image.

Opposite **Hubert Hilscher,** *Cyrk*, **poster, Poland, 1970s** Good poster design became a source of national pride in Poland. In 1962, concern over the quality of design in circus posters saw a jury selection of twelve designs a year published by Graphic Arts Publishers in Warsaw, and the first International Poster Biennial was held in 1964. A focus on illustration and bright colours typify this upbeat work.

Right **F. H. K. Henrion, *Stop Nuclear Suicide*, poster for the Campaign for Nuclear Disarmament, UK, 1960** The Campaign for Nuclear Disarmament was founded in 1958 to promote peaceful protest against the use of nuclear weapons. In this promotional poster, Henrion created a photomontage showing a skull against a mushroom cloud. It was overprinted using black on yellow, giving it an ominous, polluted feel. The poster was banned on the basis that it encouraged political controversy, and London Transport refused to permit it to be displayed on the grounds that the image was too disturbing. Henrion's best-known work was for large-scale corporate identity programmes. The CND symbol shown here was designed by Gerald Holtom.

Below right **Grapus, *Untitled*, poster, France, 1976** This poster combines the Viet Cong flag with the smiling face of a young Vietnamese girl to celebrate the end of the war in Indo-China in 1975. It was produced by Grapus, an alliance of designers established in France in the wake of the student / worker uprising in Paris in 1968. Members of the group were first involved with the Atelier Populaire, a studio based at the École Nationale Supérieure des Beaux-Arts that produced work in support of the protests.

Opposite above **Jamie Reid, *God Save the Queen*, album cover for the Sex Pistols, UK, 1977** A tradition of subversion in design continued in the 1970s with the visual language hatched by the disillusioned, alienated and disaffected punk generation. The performance of punk music was ad hoc and aggressive, and the recorded music was equally raw. Jamie Reid's use of torn paper, disregard for typographic convention and inversion of traditional symbols screamed out in opposition to mainstream music graphics and slick corporate design, offending traditional social values.

Opposite below **Hipgnosis, *Dark Side of the Moon*, album cover for Pink Floyd, UK, 1973** Storm Thorgerson, Aubrey Powell and Peter Christopherson, members of the Hipgnosis design group, specialized in the design of album covers. Their designs for Pink Floyd frequently used photography to create enigmatic imagery that reflected the content of the album and appealed to the band's audience. The cover for *Dark Side of the Moon* shows a refracting prism drawn by George Hardie, calling to mind the spectacular light shows at the band's concerts. A concept album, it explored the nature of human experience.

STOP NUCLEAR SUICIDE CAMPAIGN FOR NUCLEAR DISARMAMENT 2 CARTHUSIAN ST LONDON EC1

4.2

Humour and Rationality

While a strong interest in revivalism and the ornamental emerged, the modernist approach continued to thrive, making the design scene truly pluralistic. This period saw the continued influence of the International and New York styles combined with more local sensibilities. British, Japanese and Dutch graphics saw the stylistic objectivity of late modernism applied alongside more specific cultural tendencies to produce distinct groups of work.

Visual Elements

_ Humour and wit in advertising and design

_ Plurality in the approach to type but often a preference for sans serif faces and a concern with new technologies

_ Holistic approach to type and image

_ Bright colours and overprinting

Right **Herb Lubalin and Tom Carnase, *Avant Garde*, typeface, US, 1968–70** Lubalin's work is known for its wit, and for its rejection of the functionalist tradition. He revelled in the features that made letterforms distinctive. His *Avant Garde* typeface, distinguished by its unusual use of ligatures in capital letters, was originally designed as a masthead for the magazine of the same name and was later developed into a full typeface by Tom Carnase. Shown here is Linotype's *ITC Avant Garde Gothic*.

Opposite **The Foundry / Wim Crouwel, *Architype Neu Alphabet*, *Architype Stedelijk* and *Architype Catalogue*, typefaces, 1960–90s** The 1960s saw the development of the first computer type, or 'optical character reading'. Just as modernist typefaces were conceived as a suitable visual language for the Machine Age, the Dutch designer Wim Crouwel was interested in the impact this new computer technology would have on typeface design. Crouwel's *Neu Alphabet* (1967) was designed using rectangular shapes to construct letterforms and can be understood as a new form of machine aesthetic. This was his most radical experiment, conceived in response to his experience of the first electronic typesetting device, with characters specifically designed to follow the underlying dot-matrix system. In 1997, The Foundry extended the typeface used by Crouwel on his *Vormgevers* poster for the Stedelijk Museum in Amsterdam. With Crouwel's input, numerals and additional characters were designed and released as *Architype Stedelijk*. *Architype Catalogue* originates from Crouwel's 1970 Stedelijk Museum catalogue for an exhibition by the sculptor Claes Oldenburg. Crouwel based his design for the lettering used on the poster on Oldenburg's soft sculptural forms. On the original poster the initials 'S' and 'M', standing for 'Stedelijk Museum', were embossed as a reference to the subject of the exhibition. At Oldenburg's request, Crouwel later developed a whole alphabet of these letterforms. Such typefaces may now evoke a sense of early digital technology and the futurism of the time.

abcdefghijklmn
opqrstuvwxyz
ABCDEFGHIJKLMN
OPQRSTUVWXYZ
0123456789
Qq

Right **Lance Wyman, 'Mexico 68', logo for the Mexico Olympics, 1968** The Op Art movement, as represented in MOMA's 'The Responsive Eye' exhibition (1965), proved to be influential in design circles throughout the 1960s. The impact of its vibrating patterns, combined with the influence of indigenous folk art and the fortuitous crossover of the year and the traditional Olympic symbol, can be seen here in the identity design for the 1968 Mexico Olympics. This logo was only one component of a comprehensive and complex identity that had to function on several levels.

Opposite above **Ken Garland, *Galy Tots*, brochure cover for Galt Toys, UK, 1969** Garland was commissioned to produce an identity for Galts, who only began producing toys in the early 1960s despite already being well established in the field of educational supplies. The initial aim was to create a strong association between the name of the company and the new product, but by 1969 Garland felt confident enough to adopt this playful approach to the company name. This brochure cover displays the typographic wit and clever manipulation of overprinting that are so evocative of this period.

Opposite below **Alan Fletcher, 'Pirelli Slippers', advertisement, UK, 1965** British graphic design showed both Swiss and American influence, and was known for its wit. Pentagram's first incarnation was established at this time as an alliance between Alan Fletcher, Bob Gill and Colin Forbes. Their approach began with an analysis of the problem at hand, including the context in which communication was to occur. In this witty and intelligent solution for a bus poster, actual passengers became part of the image.

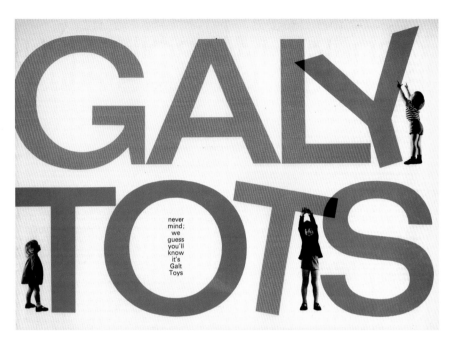

never
mind;
we
guess
you'll
know
it's
Galt
Toys

Portfolio

Our anything-goes cultural environment has seen retro work grow in scope to include a range of styles, materials and techniques. Our frames of reference have continued to shift and expand as new generations of designers have emerged, as our understanding of graphic design history has deepened and our visual literacy has continued to become more sophisticated.

This section brings together a varied selection of recent design projects inspired by a rich legacy of 150 years of graphic design. Drawn from editorial, information, branding, identity, packaging, type and promotional design, it ranges from the commercial to the cultural to the experimental. This collection of work shows creative and thoughtful interpretations of historical forms, references, processes and techniques. It demonstrates clearly that our definition of retro as a theme in design has to move beyond the narrow confines that have sometimes been ascribed to it. This strand of influence must now be seen to encompass not just a broader array of sources but also an interest in the working processes of our predecessors. A continued interest in the popular modernism of the mid-20th century requires us to develop a deeper understanding of its use, and the expanding variety of influences which are now apparent demands new discussion. So here, alongside some more familiar interpretations, is work that looks to the seemingly timeless technology of letterpress, exuberant Victorian typography, modernist fonts and imagery, the layered references of psychedelia or the objectivity of the International Style for inspiration. These sources are often combined with other influences to create satisfying and stimulating graphic solutions.

Where possible, the designers' own words have been included to give a more direct sense of what each piece is trying to achieve. Unless otherwise stated, quotes that appear in captions for new work are taken from the designers' comments.

Editorial Design in both traditional and digital media plays a central role in the transmission of knowledge and ideas. It has always provided a platform for high-quality and experimental approaches and continues to be a prized vehicle of expression for designers. While covers act as packaging for the ideas and stories that lie within, and as such must grab the attention of the consumer, other aspects of the design solution must communicate effectively and maintain the reader's interest. It must speak to both a broad target audience and the consumer as an individual. The image and typography must be responsive to the content of the text, giving expression to its voice.

The development of graphic design itself is rooted in the history of books. As material objects, they have a special meaning – there is a relationship between the consumer and the book as a tactile thing that has survived despite the alternatives presented to us by technology. Put simply, people keep books. As historical things, they seem to become particularly evocative of their own times, perhaps because of the nature of their content, the immediacy of their design or the wealth of good work that this field has produced. That may be why some of the most successful contemporary design solutions have looked to the history of book design itself for inspiration. For example, the Penguin Great Ideas series calls on key aspects of its own archive as well as inspiration gleaned from further afield to operate both individually and as a collection of 'special' objects, while other projects have taken an entirely different route.

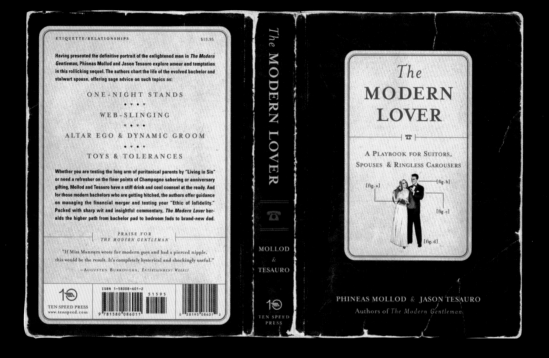

ETIQUETTE/RELATIONSHIPS $15.95

Having presented the definitive portrait of the enlightened man in *The Modern Gentleman*, Phineas Mollod and Jason Tesauro explore amour and temptation in this rollicking sequel. The authors chart the life of the evolved bachelor and stalwart spouse, offering sage advice on such topics as:

ONE-NIGHT STANDS

♦ ♦ ♦

WEB-SLINGING

♦ ♦ ♦

ALTAR EGO & DYNAMIC GROOM

♦ ♦ ♦

TOYS & TOLERANCES

Whether you are testing the long arm of puritanical parents by "Living in Sin" or need a refresher on the finer points of Champagne sabering or anniversary gifting, Mollod and Tesauro have a stiff drink and cool counsel at the ready. And for those modern bachelors who are getting hitched, the authors offer guidance on managing the financial merger and testing your "Ethic of Infidelity." Packed with sharp wit and insightful commentary, *The Modern Lover* heralds the higher path from bachelor pad to bedroom fads to brand-new dad.

PRAISE FOR
THE MODERN GENTLEMAN

"If Miss Manners wrote for modern guys and had a pierced nipple, this would be the result. It's completely hysterical and shockingly useful."
—AUGUSTEN BURROUGHS, *ENTERTAINMENT WEEKLY*

ISBN 1-58008-601-2

TEN SPEED PRESS
www.tenspeed.com

9 781580 086011

The
The MODERN LOVER

MOLLOD
&
TESAURO

TEN SPEED
PRESS

The
MODERN
LOVER

A PLAYBOOK FOR SUITORS,
SPOUSES & RINGLESS CAROUSERS

[fig. a]   [fig. b]

[fig. c]

[fig. d]

PHINEAS MOLLOD & **JASON TESAURO**
Authors of *The Modern Gentleman*

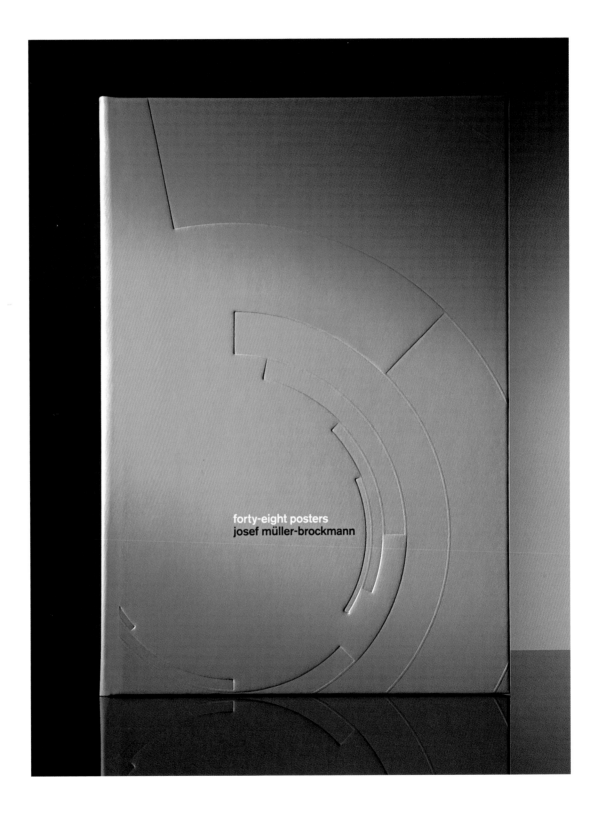

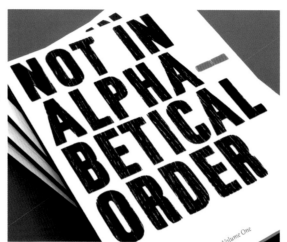

Opposite **Image Now, Josef Müller-Brockmann: Forty-eight Posters, exhibition catalogue. Client: Image Now Gallery** To document an exhibition of posters by Müller-Brockmann, Image Now chose to create a new piece of design in the spirit of the Swiss designer's approach. The cover of the catalogue is a simple homage to one of his best-known and most complex graphic arrangements; it echoes the poster illustration for a recital of Beethoven's 'Coriolanus' Overture (1955). The illustration was blind-embossed on to the cover of an A5 casebound book. The intention was to create the feel of a minimalist testament to a master craftsman. This concept was echoed inside the book through tributes paid to Müller-Brockmann's legacy by contemporary international designers.

This page **Atelier David Smith, *Not In Alphabetical Order*, Fingal Public Art Collection, Volume 1. Client: Fingal County Council** According to the designer, the title, *Not in Alphabetical Order*, refers to the organic nature of how this public art collection was assembled. This approach is reflected also in the cataloguing and documentation of the work. It was the intuitive, 'hands-on' nature of collecting that informed the decision to print woodblocks for the cover and headline text. The custom headline type is loosely based on the proportions of *Univers Condensed* to complement the book's text face. The typographic panels were laser cut into beech-veneered MDF and hand-printed at the Graphic Studio, Dublin by master printmaker, Tom Phelan. The signature red was printed as a special throughout.

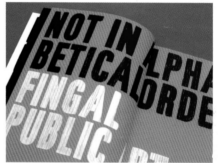

**Brenda Dermody, poetry book
covers. Client: Salmon Poetry**
The visual approach to the design of
this series of poetry collections takes
inspiration from American advertising
illustration of the 1950s. The soft colour
palette and eclectic mix of typefaces
reinforce the overall retro feel of the set.

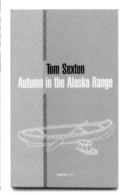

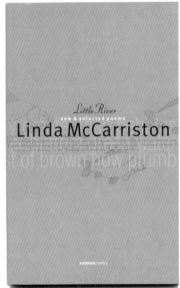

Right **Unreal, book covers. Uncorrected proof for *The Night Watch*. Client: Virago / Times Warner Books;** *Centre right* **The Radioactive Boyscout, Client: 4th Estate;** *Below* **Fatland. Client: Penguin** In their design for the proof cover of *The Night Watch*, Unreal used a combination of script (*Jackson Script*) and sans serif (*Corpius*) typefaces to recall the 1940s. The cover for *The Radioactive Boyscout* parodies the same era through its use of type and image. On the cover for *Fatland*, a book about obesity in America, they used the visual language of consumerism to communicate its content.

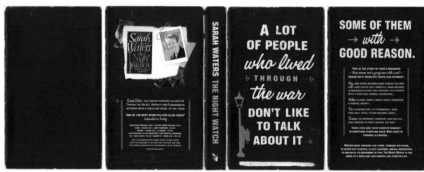

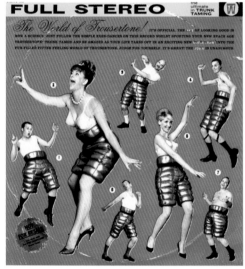

Above left and centre **Mark Denton Design, *D&AD Annual 2004*. Client: British Design and Art Direction (D&AD)** David Dye art-directed the 2004 *D&AD Annual*. His concept was to base the design on classic album covers and commission various designers to style the individual jury pages. Mark Denton Design produced a spoof 'dancercise' record sleeve in the style of vernacular design of the 1950s. The 'record' was to be given away with a pair of inflatable exercise pants.

Atelier Works, Eye to Eye Book Covers. Client: The British Council

The Birthday Counterpoints, a series of books exploring different aspects of cultural identity and interaction, was published to mark the seventieth birthday of the British Council. Atelier Works' Quentin Newark began the design process for this set of covers by trying to define culture as a concept: 'What is culture? It seems so big that it has no shape, no one idea, it's almost too big to define. But then we realized it's always happening to and stemming from people. We have to depict people in some way. (But with no budget for photography.) Immediately I started drawings using the face since a face can stand as a synechdoche, part for a whole. Each cover came quite quickly, burgers for cultural imperialism, painted faces for nationalism.

'There is a natural tendency for me to go back in time to the sixties. The combination in that era of bright flat colour, crisp geometric forms, and sans serif type is one I find endlessly attractive and powerful. And that era was deeply wrapped up in overt politics. You cannot look at material from those decades without feeling the pressure of Socialism in all its forms, declaring itself in the bluntness and unequivocalness of the graphics ... The subject matter of the logo [see page 166] and the books is ultimately about a search for clarity, and the style seemed a natural underpinning for this work.'

BRITISH COUNCIL | 70 TH ANNIVERSARY 1934 – 2004

Trust me,
I'm a scientist

Birthday Counterpoints

Pervez Hoodebhoy, Dan Glaser, Steven Shapin

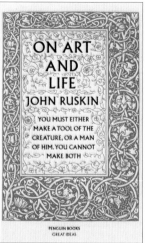

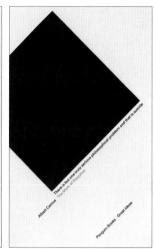

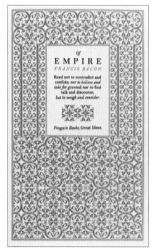

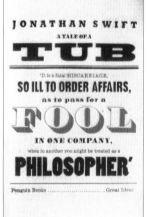

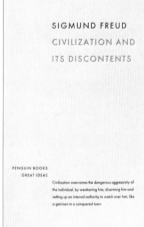

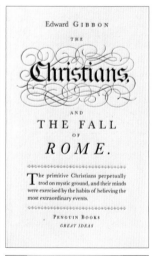

Penguin In-house with Phil Baines, Catherine Dixon, Alistair Hall, Great Ideas. Client: Penguin Books Although they have become comparatively rare in publishing – most book covers sport an image – Penguin has a rich history of purely typographic cover designs. Thus when deciding on a type-based direction for the Great Ideas series, the in-house art director Jim Stoddart and designer David Pearson felt that the cumulative effect of the series of twenty covers would give the titles sufficient presence when displayed. This approach had been used to great effect by previous Penguin designers Derek Birdsall and David Pelham. The typefaces for each design varied from the traditional to more contemporary interpretations of classic faces. Some of the lettering was also hand-rendered. The debossed off-white paper that is soft to the touch references the tactile nature of letterpress printing. As a final touch Pearson replaced the Penguin logo on many of the covers with text to add to the period feel.

Pearson describes the typographic approach as follows: 'At this early stage the typefaces were not strictly faithful to the period of each title, but rather a loose interpretation of it. I think the set could have easily turned into a straight-laced, visual history of lettering but I found that half the fun of the design process was finding more abstract and non-literal links to the subject matter. This seemed to give the project a little humour. It also meant that bringing in and briefing the other designers was a much more enjoyable process.' In the second generation of twenty Penguin Great Ideas, blue replaced red as the second colour. Pearson describes the approach to repackaging this way: 'I think that classic literature constantly has to be looked at in terms of its packaging. Are we happy to restrict the circulation of these texts to academics alone, or can we break them out and offer them to new audiences? Classic texts have withstood the test of time so a modern design approach feels just as appropriate as a traditional one.'

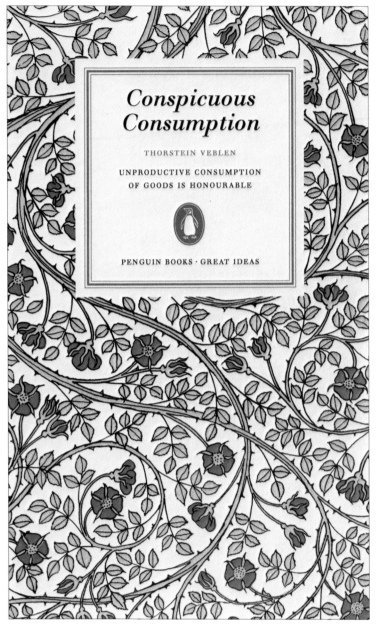

Conspicuous Consumption

THORSTEIN VEBLEN

UNPRODUCTIVE CONSUMPTION
OF GOODS IS HONOURABLE

PENGUIN BOOKS · GREAT IDEAS

From top left **Pocket Penguins. Sue Townsend, designer: D*Face, *The Queen in Hell Close*; Antony Beevor, designer: Nathan Burton, *Christmas at Stalingrad*; Regina V, designer: Nathan Burton, *Lady Chatterly's Trial*; J. K. Galbraith, designer: Alan Aldridge, *The Economics of Innocent Fraud*; John Updike, designer: Romek Marber, *Three Trips*; Roald Dahl, designer: Billie Jean, *A Taste of the Unexpected*. Client: Penguin Books**

These covers from the Pocket Penguins series art-directed by Jim Stoddart and John Hamilton show another return to the legacy of Penguin cover design. Many of the designs reference illustrative and typographic styles from the last seventy years. In this small range of examples we see references to album-cover design, design from the 1960s to the 1980s, and a new take on the 1960s conceptual image.

D*face describes the influences for *The Queen in Hell Close*: 'As a kid I grew up listening to punk music, skateboarding and doing graffiti. A strong link between all these cultures is a DIY ethic, from the band made sleeve art to skater drawn board graphics to the zines that accompanied them all. One of the key artists at this time was Jamie Reid, his cut and paste artwork visually articulated the music of the time perfectly. The use of the queen on a union jack with a safety pin through her nose was a powerful image which fitted Johnny Rotten's voice of dissent perfectly. With Reid's Queen as a reference firmly wedged in my mind, I used my much propagated wings and tongue graphic to add a further tongue in cheek poke at the establishment.'

The jacket for *Christmas in Stalingrad* by Penguin in-house designer Nathan Burton was inspired by Soviet propaganda posters of the period: 'After reading the piece it seemed that this was a natural way for the design to be led. I have always found [the posters] to be brutally beautiful so it was a great opportunity to create my own homage to the genre. Black and red is a recurring colour scheme from the posters so it was the natural choice. The image was made by layering solid colour bit-maps to give the overprinted / textured quality. The lettering was scanned from old type specimen books.'

The cover for Dahl's *A Taste of the Unexpected* looks to the work of Robert Rauschenberg and Eduardo Paolozzi. Illustrator Billie Jean describes how it is '[p]redominantly limited to blue biro drawings, there is a confluence of different images styles and patterns ...' Other influences here included the Pop Art hand lettering of Sister Corita Kent: 'I find the rhythm colour and playfulness of her work really inspiring,' says Jean.

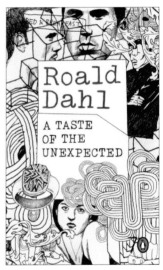

Peter Mendelsund, book covers.
Client: Alfred A. Knopf Publishers

Peter Mendelsund describes his approach to designing *The Anatomy of Fascism* as follows: 'I wanted to make an Albert Speer [piece]. Now if ever there was a Fascist font, *Futura* seems to me to fit the bill. Muscular and clean, it seems to be a face Speer could have loved. Extruding the letterforms was my own little way of adding some extra monumentality to an already monumental font. I had to throw in a blackletter as well. The triangular shape seemed to echo the theme of Fascism. The colour was just my own whimsy.' For *K.* he describes how the cover design 'is in its own way, an example of the constructivist aesthetic ... the photographic repetition of Kafka's photo was a technique employed often by Rodchenko and others.'

On the cover for *¡Caramba!* the intention was to recreate 'the Mexican street-art aesthetic of the novel. The fonts used are *Kavaler Cursive* – which has been manipulated to look as though it was printed off-register – *Signpainter*, *Clarendon MT* and *Commercial Script MT'*. Mendelsund carried this approach inside the book by using type and illustration as though they had been 'set badly and printed on shoddy presses'.

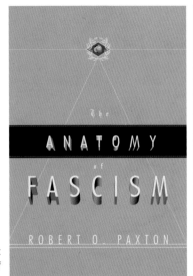

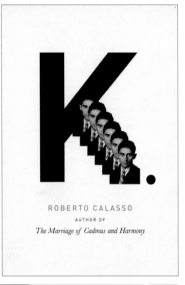

Atelier Works, *Royal Society of the Arts Annual Review 2001.* **Client: Royal Society of Arts** The concept for the *Royal Society of Arts Annual Review* is outlined by Atelier Works: 'No one would invent the Royal Society of Arts in our era. Its mission "to encourage arts, manufactures and commerce" seems so ambitious and generous in its vision of an interdependent culture. We are completely demarcated today – when does a scientist ever talk with a typographer, or a CEO with a painter? In our design work for the RSA, we used the idea of multiplicity and expressed it in different ways; through typefaces, formats, sub-identities, paper stocks, and so on. The tone is always the binding factor: a low-key, elegant, worldly intelligence.

'The *Annual Review* is a detailed text, it is animated and enriched with different typographic illustrations from the RSA's own Royal Designers for Industry: Alan Fletcher, John McConnell, Mike Dempsey, Pierre Mendell, Derek Birdsall, Malcolm Garrett, Alan Kitching. The inventiveness and enduring quality of these respected designers embody the RSA's principle of honouring diverse approaches.

'Aimed primarily at RSA sponsors and Fellows, it is also to be used to nurture high powered opinion formers who often don't have time to read. Being a charity, the design had to tread between looking too corporate, with an extravagant design or looking in much need of sponsorship with a compromised design. The result is short, uncluttered and discursive.'

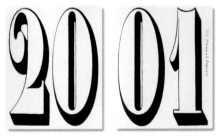

HarrimanSteel, *Rubbish Fashion Annual.* **Client: Rubbish** In these spreads HarrimanSteel refer to an eclectic range of visual styles from the 1920s onwards: 'Rubbish is a fashion annual looking at the silly side of style. It is an antidote to all of the high-brow fashion publications who take themselves far too seriously. *Rubbish* is loosely inspired by the annuals of our childhoods from the late 1960s to the early 1980s: the *Beano*, *Bunty*, and *Whizzer and Chips*, for example. Inspiration was also taken from advertising of the 1950s and from publications like *The Chap*.' The cover is printed on gloss-coated board with a foil-blocked masthead. Hardbound and sewn, it has glued endpapers and a round spine with head and tail bands.

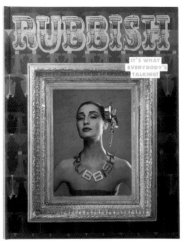

**Vasava, cover and editorial illustrations.
Client: La Vanguardia Sunday
Magazine** These illustrations were
commissioned for an issue of *La Vanguardia*'s
Sunday supplement entitled *Generation
2006*. This special edition featured articles
about contemporary youth culture in Spain.
Vasava wanted the cover illustration to
convey the idea that young Spanish women
are at the heart of this culture. The flowing
lines of the hair are intended to evoke a
tree; images of the interests and concerns
of this generation – travel, music, technology,
relationships and so on – are entwined in
the branches. This theme is continued
across the series of images. The illustrations
contain layered references from past styles,
including Art Nouveau.

Right **Morla Design, *Hemispheres*
magazine. Client: United Airlines**
Morla Design created the April 2002
cover of *Hemispheres,* United Airlines
award-winning in-flight magazine,
describing it as 'Neo-Modern in feel …
a playful combination of ellipses and
circles'. It recalls Alexander Calder's
mobiles of the 1950s.
Below **Marlin, editorial illustrations.
Client: *Men's Health Magazine*** These
editorial illustrations accompanied an
article in *Men's Health Magazine* about
how to promote yourself in the workplace.
To quote Marlin, 'Inspired by classic
campaign buttons, the illustrations have
a collectable retro look with just enough
scratches and bottom-of-the drawer
dings to look authentic and still be
readable.' The messages were drawn
from popular American political jargon
and historic campaign slogans.

Headcase Design, *The Modern Lover: A Playbook for Suitors, Spouses & Ringless Carousers*. Client: Ten Speed Press According to Headcase, '*The Modern Lover* offers sage advice and savoir-faire for bachelors, spouses and fathers. The visual treatment of the book was really just an extension of the author's voice. The cover quotes a well-worn little black book, hinting at the prospect of romantic conquests, while the retro image overlaid with diagrammatic graphic elements underscores the idea of tried-and-true information being presented with a modern twist.' Headcase created a distressed feel throughout the book to give the impression of a well-thumbed volume. This effect is enhanced through the use of a traditional colour palette of red and black printed on an off-white stock.

This is followed through inside the book with 1940s and 1950s vignette-style illustrations and diagrams, including one showing the angle and point of contact for sabering a bottle of champagne. This combination of dry instructional graphics with retro imagery creates tongue-in-cheek humour. The intention is to take the reader back to a time when dating and romance were seen with much less cynicism.

Sid Lee, 'Alexis de Portneuf'. Client: Saputo Following its acquisition of Fromagerie Caron and Fromagerie Cayer, Saputo sought to create a combined branding strategy that would enable it to compete more efficiently. The designer describes how 'when we purchase cheese we also purchase a piece of its history, the know-how of its artisans and the region. This is how Alexis de Portneuf was born.' Grainy black-and-white photography and evocative typography were used to build on the sense of tradition and authenticity that already surrounds the product.

Carin Goldberg Design, *Catalog.*
Client: Carin Goldberg Design
The acquisition of a 1950s mail-order catalogue from a flea market was the inspiration for Carin Goldberg's *Catalog*. It features her personal selection of some sixty objects from the thousands of products visualized in the original. Although such ephemera can recall the past in a very immediate way, placing the half-tone images in a new context creates new meaning. In the book's introduction Dorothy Twining Globus states that Goldberg was 'not attracted by the nostalgia evoked by the visions of this past era. The images she has chosen are pure forms, minimally decorative, juxtaposed to suggest further associations and ideas'. Isolating the individual images and creating high-resolution reproductions of them emphasize their original qualities. Goldberg used a muted colour palette and referenced the 'index-style' typography of the original.

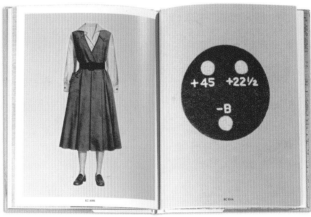

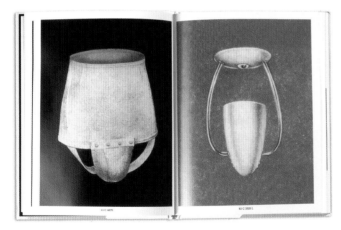

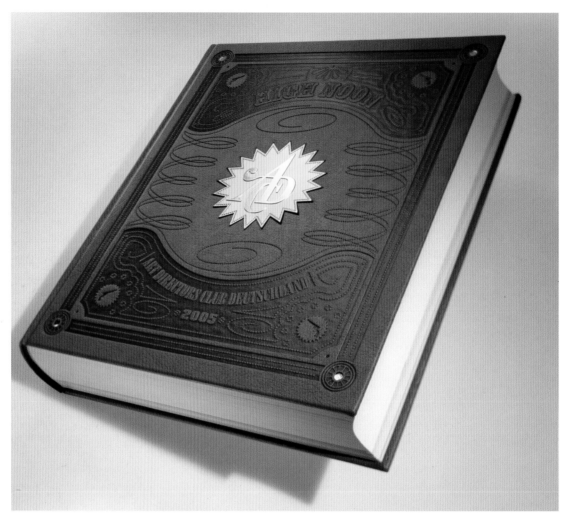

Strichpunkt, *ADC Yearbook 2005*.
Client: ADC für Deutschland Verlag
GMBH This design for the yearbook
for the Art Directors Club of Germany
aimed to recreate the atmosphere of
the American Gold Rush and Wild West.
It is a playful reference to the intense
competition that surrounds 'the annual
battle for ADC gold'. A leather cover with
metallic sheriff's star along with layouts
and imagery in the style of wanted
posters and sepia-toned photographs
were employed to achieve the effect.

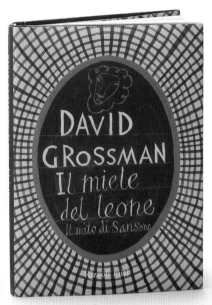

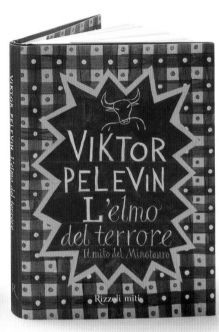

Mucca Design, The Myth Series. Illustrator:
Jeff Fisher. Client: Rizzoli Rizzoli Myths (Rizzoli Miti)
is a project involving twenty-five editors from around
the world who are collecting modern interpretations
of epic myths. Mucca states that '…the design borrows
from the visual language of traditional bookmaking'.
The covers recall patterned endpapers used in the
early 20th century.

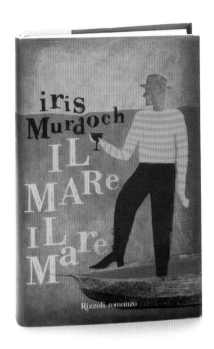

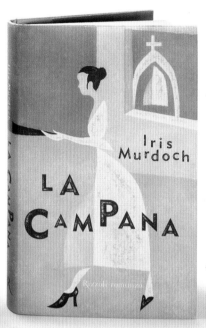

Mucca Design, Iris Murdoch Series. Illustrator: Dennis Clouse: Cyclone Design. Client: Rizzoli

The illustrations used in Mucca Design's covers for this Iris Murdoch series are reminiscent of the reductive imagery and colour palettes of the 1920s and 1930s. The designers wanted the visual style to 'capture an element of each individual story while uniting the books with a similar look and feel. Murdoch's stories feature richly textured characterization, so each image focuses on personality and character without being as specific as a portrait. The illustration technique borrows from various sources without distinctly referencing one in particular, including the worn hand-painted signage of a carnival midway and flat colour shapes reminiscent of the work of Matisse.'

Atelier David Smith, *'Hard Things in a Hard Place'*, William H. Walsh lecture. Client: Institute of Designers in Ireland (IDI) This publication celebrates the first in a series of annual IDI design lectures. The inaugural lecture commemorated William H. Walsh, the founder of the multidisciplinary Kilkenny Design Workshops. Smith's design uses a combination of bright colours and overprinting. While consistent with the bold colour combinations typical of 1960s interiors and graphics, the colour treatment also served to mask the inferior quality of the many second-generation images and documentation used in the design which date from the workshop's foundation.

**Atelier David Smith, *Blake & Sons*.
Client: Lewis Glucksman Gallery** This book features critical essays and a number of works by international artists created in response to the legacy of the English artist William Blake. The designer David Smith looks to the precision of fine typography and restrained colourways of traditional book design. In this instance, according to Smith '… the book is completely set in Stanley Morison's *Times New Roman*, a design decision that acknowledges the "Englishness" of the content.'

Through his conflation of classical and medieval motifs, Romantic and neo-classical elements, Blake attempted to create an alternative visual language for his alternative vision.[8] The ideology of Blake's visual language attempted to re-form, or rather transform, the English Identity. This is evident in the prints from *Europe a Prophecy*, particularly plates 6 and 7, where Blake depicts England under the conditions of both plague and famine. The mental and spiritual transformations of *Europe a Prophecy* examine, through an allegorical manner, contemporary British and European politics, particularly the restrictions imposed upon England from 1793, a year before the publication of *Europe a Prophecy*. The overt political quietism of the prints reflects the conservative nationalism dominating social and political discourse in England.

Inspired by a vision that Blake encountered while living in Lambeth[9], the frontispiece of *Europe a Prophecy, The Ancient of Days*, is a remarkable fusion of Christian, Classical, and mythological motifs. Although printed in 1821, this relief etching and watercolour trembles on the edge of a modernist aesthetic, 'primitive' and "crude" formal composition gestures towards the wood engraving of the German expressionists.[10] Allegory and wholly anti-naturalistic, *Europe a Prophecy* is a print full of oppositions and contrasts, due to the dialectical quality, it contains "its own antithesis". The viewer encounters the figure of Urizen, performing the supremely rational act of dividing and inscribing the world. The form of Urizen, in tandem with the act, is described in Blake's pen, ink and watercolour work *Newton* (c. 1795). Absorbed and enthralled in their own action, both the figures of Newton and Urizen represent closure, rejecting "imagination: the divine vision".[11]

In his book *Blake and Context*, Crehan demonstrates the "anti-rational, […] ironic visual language".[12] Through a conscious distortion of both anatomy and colour, Blake demonstrates how the geometrical nature of the figure of Urizen stands in opposition to the irrationality of the formal elements. The visual language of Blake's prints rail against and eschew the Newtonian vision of a finite nature, a nature imprisoned by empirical activity. Rather, the luminous colour of Urizen, and the altered and disfigured anatomy, draws attention to the revolutionary and unsettling aspects of the print. Thus, as Stewart Crehan outlines, Blake's use of both implicit irony and satire in his works challenge the language of empiricism, and attempt to transcend their own historical conditions: The function of Blake's visual language […] is ironic and satiric. The first impression conveyed by *The Ancient of the days* is one of divine creative power, but this is negated by the 'minute particulars' and underlying irony of the whole design. Urizen is not a 'God' at all; nor is he creative. He is merely the 'Supreme Being' of rational theology who resides in the breasts of the dominant class. Blake's visual language opposes as well as exposes the profound irrationality of a governing Reason that tries to make the infinite finite; binds what cannot be bound, and with terrible compulsion keeps on measuring what cannot be measured.[13]

The "minute particulars" of Urizen highlight the subversive and transgressive aspects of Blake's print, and although bound and hidden in the complex and private iconography of the artist, Blake's symbolism demonstrates his revolutionary attitude. By negating the "divine creative power" of Urizen and therefore exposing the follies of the dominant class, Blake produces a profoundly powerful and complex political

visual paradigm, to which the marginalised, and the socially oppressed, may cling to, if they wish, in order to raise and activate their downtrodden selves.

The ironic and satirical elements present in Blake's frontispiece find their counterpoint in much of the other work in the exhibition. Irony, often a meta-strategy of the postmodernist surfaces in the video work of Paul Chan. Chan's video piece, *Now let Us Praise American Leftists* (2000) is the only directly political work in the exhibition. Ironic and playfully sinister in its framing and editing technique[14], Chan juxtaposes the eyeless faces, which embody their own ideologies and with a voice over of the text *In these Great Times*, written by Karl Kraus in 1914. Although polemic in tone, the ambiguity and irony of the work reflects the attitude in the frontispiece of Blake's *Europe a Prophecy* (for a moment, we may imagine that the disembodied voice in the video is that of Urizen). While formally the work demonstrates a nostalgia for an out-moded form, the editing technique gestures dialectally to the current proliferation of images and the dissolution of a stable identity: two of the central strategies of postmodern practice.

In tandem to Crehan's reading of the frontispiece of *Europe a Prophecy*, Anthony Blunt's essay "The Ancient of Days" examines the significance of the compass, and its historical trajectory, of the figure of Urizen. Blunt lucidly demonstrates the duality of the print and shows how the figure of Urizen represented all that Blake loathed in the materialism of his day. Urizen symbolizes the end to creative imagination, the compass, a sign of division, separation, and ultimately, Newtonian rationalism. The energy of the print, confined in the vivid colour of Urizen, deconstructs the act. "Who shall bind the infinite?"[15] The anti-rationalist doctrine that permeate the pages of *Europe a Prophecy* returns to surface in work of Sam Basu, David Thorpe, Kenneth Anger, and David Altmejd. Through a variety of different mediums, these artists continue to probe the central issues that surface in Blake's philosophy.

One other oppositional strategy present in *Europe a Prophecy*, which I alluded to above, was Blake's use of medieval iconography. The imagery of Plate 5 in *Europe a*

1 Rosalind Krauss, *The Cultural Logic of the Late Capitalist Museum*, Massachusetts: October, Vol. 54 Autumn, MIT Press, 1990, p. 3.
2 Ibid, p. 3.
3 Ibid, p. 5.
4 Stephan Eisenman, ed, *Nineteenth Century Art: A Critical History*, London: Thames & Hudson, p. 163.
5 Craske Matthew, *Art in Europe*, Oxford: Oxford University Press, 1997, pp. 7-21.
6 Brian Lukacher, p. 132.
7 This phrase originates in the writings of Samuel Beckett. However, Beckett railed against the ambitions of the "gentle reader", and not the "gentle viewer". In this context, I think the alteration is warranted.
8 Plate 5 and 15 of *Europe a Prophecy* demonstrate this conflation and allegation of seemingly opposing visual languages.
9 Anthony Blunt, *Blake's 'Ancient of Days': The Symbolism of the Compass*, New York: Journal of Warburg Institute, Vol. 2, No. 1, July, 1938, pp. 53-63.
10 Both the words "primitive" and "crude" arise in contemporary criticism of Blake's work. See: Stewart Crehan, *Blake in Context*, London: Gill and Macmillan, 1984, pp. 192-239.
11 William Blake quoted in, *The Art of William Blake*, Columbia: Columbia University Press, 1959.
12 Ibid, pp. 267
13 Stewart Crehan, p. 239.
14 Chan's presentation draws on the latest computer imaging software with which law enforcement agencies use to identify suspect terrorists and criminals.
15 Anthony Blunt, p. 96. Blunt acknowledges that the sentence appears on a first sketch of the frontispiece.

118

119

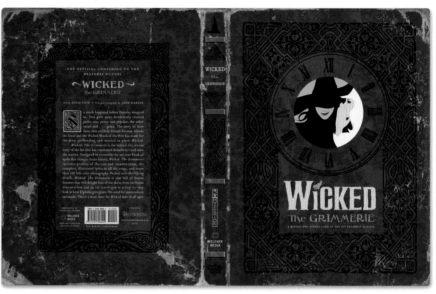

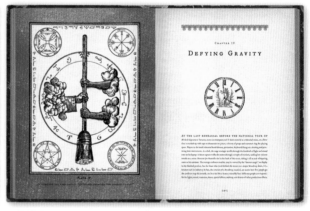

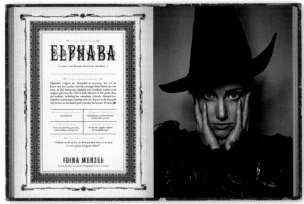

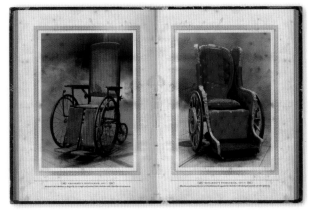

Headcase Design, *Wicked: The Grimmerie*. Client: Melcher Media

Headcase Design created this book to accompany the Broadway show *Wicked*, a revisionist look at *The Wizard of Oz*. Headcase describes the design process this way: 'The story exists in a fictional time period, but there is a decidedly Victorian look to the play (which stems from the real time period the books were written in), so this became a sort of typographic anchor for the book. Borders, flourishes and engravings from the era were also used throughout to complement the type. On certain spreads, such as the character profiles, we overprinted several layers of borders and employed more fanciful display fonts in order to convey the over-the-top whimsy of the play. For other sections, when legibility was more of a concern, we looked to 19th century book design for inspiration, integrating such elements as symmetrically-oriented dingbats,

illustrative initial caps, and fonts with antiquated ligatures.

'Our primary goal was to create the ultimate keepsake for fans of the show, so we wanted to make it look like the ancient spell book of the main character, Elphaba (the Wicked Witch of the West). To this end we painstakingly aged each page of the book. We scanned in a large assortment of pages from old books that had stains, holes, yellowing and other types of damage to the paper. We then layered these over each spread in Photoshop and used layer masks to reveal various types of distress, striving to keep them as different as possible on each spread.

'We researched archaic texts on magic, such as *The Key of Solomon*, and incorporated design elements from the various "seals" found throughout these books. One reason these look so authentic is the use of runic letterforms, which come across as a secret, unknown

language. There was also use of some Hebrew typography to give the chapter openers an almost Kabbalistic feel. We then juxtaposed those elements with illustrations from the original *Oz* series (which fortunately for us, due to their age, are in the public domain) to create a look that captured the whimsical yet dark tone of the play. John R. Neill's wonderful drawings were a nice complement to the Victorian aspect of the book. We really liked the texture of the old litho printing, and tried to pick that up whenever possible, particularly in overlaying black line art over solid green. As in the play, the colour green was a theme throughout the book, contrasting Elphaba's skin tone (which many believed was the cause of her alleged wickedness) with the glamour of the Emerald City.'

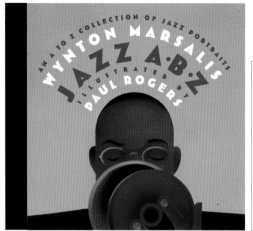

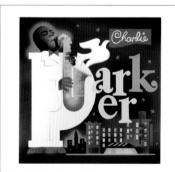

**Paul Rogers, *Jazz ABZ*. Illustrator: Jill von
Hartmann. Client: Candlewick Press** Evocative
combinations of type and image in the style of the Jazz
Age were used to create the illustrations for *Jazz ABZ*.
This book is the result of a collaboration between the
designer / illustrator Paul Rogers and the musician
Wynton Marsalis, serving as both an introduction and
a tribute to twenty-six jazz greats from 'A' to 'Z'. The
designer Jill von Hartmann felt that '… Marsalis's poetry
and Rogers's illustrations had to be presented in a
format that was accurate, elegant and sophisticated.
In order to mimic the hand-crafted graphic design
of jazz music's golden age, all of the illustrations were
created with traditional materials (paint on board).
Influences included Alex Steinweiss, Jim Flora, Paul
Rand, Miguel Covarrubias and David Stone Martin, as
well as other significant graphic designers and artists
of the 20th century. The visual styles for the album
cover-like illustrations were chosen to reflect the era
in which the musician was most prominent.

'The book was bound in the style of an old '78 record
album, including the Kraft paper endpapers die-cut to
look like a record sleeve on the inside front cover.'

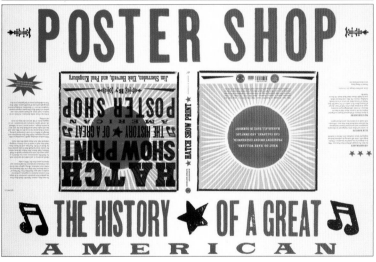

Hatch Show Print, *Hatch Show Print: The History of a Great American Poster Shop.* **Client: Chronicle Books** Hatch Show Print's Jim Sherraden describes the design process for the cover of their monograph: 'We gave the publisher several different versions of the book cover. The piece they chose is a direct tribute to the classical Hatch style. This started with the first layer being the sunburst, hand brayered in two colours, which is a constant and a proven attention grabber … The typefaces I chose were to celebrate the grand tradition of the original Gothic (sans serif) typefaces. This is accented with a typeface designed by William Page in the late 1880s. I was told by Mr Hatch's nephew that this was in the original bank of typefaces purchased by his uncle when he took the shop over in the early 1920s. For that reason alone I was compelled to use it in the book cover, for the word "Hatch".'

Sherraden goes on to describe how '… the rest of the cover is fleshed out with *Bodoni Bold* and *Tower*. (By the way, I notice that my young staff call some of the typefaces by different names, that they probably learned from computer programs, but I'm sticking with the original titles and continue my endeavor to brainwash them with true letterpress history.) Of course I added a few of the usual dingbats and music notes, again celebrating the richness of this letterpress archive. At Hatch Show Print we have a passion for both our history, and what we do with the present. We hope this book cover is a primary example of the joys of letterpress.' The front cover is shown top left while the image below it shows the full effect of the unfolded dustjacket.

Packaging Design must be one of the aspects of graphic design most often encountered by consumers. Like almost all visual communication, it has to operate on both functional and symbolic levels. It seems that sifting through a deluge of packaging is an inevitable part of contemporary life. However, a well-conceived design can also offer the possibility of escape. Retro style often participates in giving packaging this special value, whether on the supermarket shelf or in a more sophisticated environment. Packaging design for food and drink products in particular seems to gravitate towards the use of retro style, perhaps aiming to recall times when traditional production processes were used or to evoke childhood memories of home comforts. Cosmetic packaging, on the other hand, often looks to the glamour of previous eras. Storytelling is a device used to lend authenticity to a product, whether relaying a real or an imagined history. The opportunities offered by the tactile and three-dimensional aspect of packaging are frequently exploited by designers to evoke a sense of the past. This section shows some examples of this process, including pressed-glass bourbon bottles, letterpressed wine labels and a contemporary fashion label packaged in silkscreened 19th-century-style cake boxes.

HENRY'S DRIVE
2003 RESERVE SHIRAZ

THIS ELEGANT WINE DISPLAYS A BOUQUET OF ROSES AND
VIOLETS. THE PALATE IS FULL OF CHOCOLATE, LICORICE
AND SPICE. VELVETY FRUIT AND FINE LONG TANNINS COMBINE
TO CREATE A SILKY, SEAMLESS STRUCTURE. THE WINE WAS
BARREL FERMENTED AND THEN MATURED IN AMERICAN OAK.
WINEMAKERS: SARAH AND SPARKY MARQUIS

BOTTLE 224 NUMBER

Henry's Drive
2003 Reserve Shiraz
Padthaway Australia

1 1/2 L

PRODUCT OF AUSTRALIA

CONTAINS SULFITES
HODGSON'S RD, PADTHAWAY SA 5271
16.0% ALC./VOLUME
IMPORTED BY THE GRATEFUL PALATE,
OXNARD CA. GRATEFULPALATE.COM
1-805-472-5283

HENRY'S DRIVE

113

Left **Sandstrom, Bulleit Bourbon. Client: Seagram** Asked to design the packaging for Bulleit Bourbon, a whisky made from an old Kentucky family recipe, Sandstrom looked to whisky museums and antique dealers 'to help bring something old back to life'. The result was this distinctive glass bottle with paper and pressed-glass labelling that reflects the influence of the mid-1800s.

Below left **Lewis Moberly, Monkey Shoulder. Client: William Grant & Sons** According to Mary Lewis, the brief here was to design packaging that would intrigue the consumer through name, design and 'story'. The project was approached with the view that '… new products need grounding, particularly when a balance between modernity and tradition is required: Monkey Shoulder targets a younger, experimental consumer who nonetheless seeks "truth" in a brand.' The three monkeys used on the shoulder of the bottle represent the three single malts used in the whisky and are a play on the term 'monkey shoulder', which describes the stoop developed by malt men after continuously turning the malting barley. The designers describe how 'tension is created through the iconic, contemporary stance of the monkey device, the simple solid bottle with its heavy base and the more restrained typographic label'. The label uses a combination of sans serif and copperplate typefaces that draw on traditional label graphics, and the three-monkey symbol appears discreetly as a watermark.

DesignWorks Enterprise IG, Slate Bourbon. Client: Diageo Chicago, with its blues heritage and underground jazz clubs, continues a proud bourbon tradition. The designers of this packaging for Slate Bourbon evoked the traditional aesthetic of the bourbon bottle while also looking to the fabric of the city for inspiration. The bottle shape is based on a single brick that has been elongated to suggest the façade of a building. The heavy embossing running down the side is a nod to the city's industrial and architectural legacy. The central focus of the packaging is the coin device where a recess has been created to suggest a viewing window. These elements combine to form a strong urban interpretation of the traditional bourbon bottle.

Right **Werner Design Werks, Inc., 10 Cane Rum. Client: Moët Hennessy** Werner Design Werks, designers of 10 Cane, a new luxury rum, looked for inspiration at vintage bottles and decanters: 'We were inspired by traditional heraldic crests as a method of telling the story of Trinidad's centuries of rum-distilling expertise.' This treatment contrasts with the irreverent placement of the vivid orange glossy label. The letters *R-U-M* were embossed onto the side of the medicinal-shaped glass bottle, and the crest was screen printed to reinforce the references to Trinidad's history of rum distilling.

Below **Pearlfisher, Waitrose whisky. Client: Waitrose** The inspiration for this typographic packaging for Waitrose whisky came from the geographic origins of the product itself. Pearlfisher's Sasha Horne describes the aim of the project as being to produce a 'sense of authenticity'. The designers used a different typeface for each whisky, exploiting the range of weights and styles to convey the richness of character and storytelling integral to the positioning of the product. *Caslon* was chosen for

the Speyside label because the designers felt that its rounded curves complemented the smooth and refined flavour of the single malt. Lowercase lettering and flourishes were used along with foil-stamped drop shadows to further emphasize the qualities of age, heritage and authenticity.

By contrast, *Franklyn* was chosen to express the strong and robust character of Island whisky. This was enhanced through the use of the 'peaty' colour scheme. The individual 'personality' of each whisky within the range was emphasized by developing a uniquely shaped label for each bottle. The bottle labels and tube wraps were offset-printed in two colours: black plus a variant colour for each whisky type. The uncoated, slightly textured paper stocks were chosen to underscore the premium feel of the range by giving a warm and natural feel in the hand. Each label and tube was then hot-foil-stamped in gold to add the finishing touch.

Together Design, Thielen wines.
Illustrator: Jeff Fisher. Client: Thielen

The Thielen family has been harvesting grapes by hand and producing wine in the Moselle valley, Germany since 1874. As co-founder of the London design group Together Design, Katja Thielen undertook the project to launch Thielen in the UK. The challenge was to create a fresh new brand to counter outdated perceptions of German wine, to demonstrate the wine's artisan and inclusive nature, and to give the brand a strong, distinct personality.

At the heart of the Thielen personality is its history, its family tradition and its artisan values. This was the starting point for the design. The aim was to create a dialogue with the audience – to use conversation to introduce the wine and its stories. As Katja Thielen put it, 'One of our greatest heroes is the modernist artist Saul Steinberg. He understood human behaviour in the finest detail which gives his work its charm and humour. Our use of illustration to create the quirky Thielen "family" owes much to his work. We also found inspiration in German folk art which had the right artisan feel and gives the design a German provenance.' Visual inspiration for the logo was drawn from *Ornamente der Völker-volkskunst in Europa & Asien* by Helmuth T. Bossert (1959). Production techniques such as textured papers, embossing and foil-blocking were employed to add depth and interest to the packaging as well as a 'traditional' feel.

**Parallax Design, Henry's Drive Reserve Shiraz.
Client: Henry's Drive Vignerons** Henry's Drive
Vignerons is named after the proprietor, Henry Hill,
who owned the mail coach service from Adelaide to
Melbourne in the early 19th century. The coach would
rest and change horses on land that is now under
vines. Drawing directly from local history, the company's
identity and wine brands follow this postal theme.

Henry's Drive Reserve Shiraz is the company's
flagship product. To mark the end of each vintage,
a special release is packaged into magnums. Rather
than a paper label, a bundle of mail (complete with
envelope, postcard and ticket) is fastened to the bottle
with a rubber band. Each individual piece adds to the
story with tasting notes and mandatory information
such as alcohol volume, appellation and so on. The
handmade nature of the packaging not only speaks
about the crafting of this fine wine but also honours
the handwritten letter – an increasingly rare commodity
in these days of email and instant communication.

Printing and finishing techniques such as die cutting,
perforation, letterpress and richly textured uncoated
stocks add to the authentic and historic feel of the
printed components. Finally, a story outlining Henry
Hill's mail coach service and its historical connection
to Henry's Drive Vignerons is enamel-baked directly
onto the bottle.

Parallax Design, Silly Mid On. Illustrator: Danny Snell. Client: Jim Barry Wines Jim Barry Wines is a boutique wine producer in the Clare Valley in South Australia. Parallax Design's Matthew Remphrey outlines the story behind the design for the Silly Mid On labels: 'In the late 1990s, the company bought the last remaining piece of land in South Australia's famed wine region, Coonawarra. The block was the old Penola Cricket Ground, complete with the pitch and pavilion. The pitch has been retained, now surrounded by vines, and the pavilion is currently being refurbished as tasting cellars. The wines produced here take their visual inspiration from the great game of cricket, Silly Mid On being no exception.' As the label states, this wine pays homage to 'cricket's most dangerous fielding position, again proving the line between bravery and stupidity is indeed fine'.

It was important that the brand had instant credibility and could not be confused with cheap cricketing merchandise. Thus the game's golden era was used as a basis for inspiration. The nostalgic label mimics old cricketing cigarette cards from the 1920s, from the illustration style to the stiff poses of the subjects. Textured uncoated label stock was utilized to further the illusion. The illustrations were also finished deliberately off register to imitate the era's printing techniques. The capsule is striped blue and cream – the colours worn by Australia's first test teams to compete for the Ashes.

Rather than designing one label for Silly Mid On, three were developed illustrating the fielder's demise. Working closely with printing and labelling suppliers, the designers were able to ensure that every case of Silly Mid On includes four of each label. This has had the effect of tripling sales, with many wine consumers buying the full set rather than one bottle.

**The Designers Republic, Lovebeing
Alu-bottle. Client: Coca-Cola** TDR's
design for Coca-Cola's Lovebeing
Alu-bottle takes its inspiration from the
promotional theme's 1960s feel. Part of
a much broader campaign that included
events, multimedia and merchandise,
the bottle uses Pop Art colours, motifs
and playful type that recall the 'love-in'
atmosphere of the 1960s and 1970s.

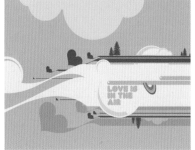
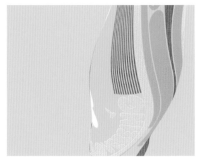

Reach, Rocombe ice-cream packaging. Client: Rocombe

Rocombe approached Reach to redesign its ice-cream packaging in order to reposition its brand. It was felt that the product was on a par with other luxury brands but that the existing packaging did not reflect its premium quality. Reach aimed to create 'an identity that reflected both the luxurious nature of the product as well as that of the target market: the affluent, professional, urban, gourmet-food lover'. The design focus was Rocombe's 'quintessential Britishness as purveyors of fine organic ice cream', with each ice cream dressed in an appropriate 'outfit' to reflect its unique flavour and personality. Classic British designs were drawn upon, like the familiar Scotch Guard's red jacket for 'Strawberries & Cream' and the clashing textures of a traditional tweed jacket worn with a silk scarf for 'Hazelnut & Praline'.

Below **Williams Murray Hamm, Curiosities packaging.**
Client: Fortnum & Mason Fortnum & Mason's 300-
year history was at the heart of the design of its flagship
Curiosities range. The products within this range are
rare, bespoke in character or only available in short
runs. The theme for the design was intended to give
the feel of a 'cabinet of curiosities', a type of collection
of strange and interesting objects and artefacts popular
in the Renaissance, and to reflect the brand's Georgian
heritage. Each piece of packaging tells an engaging
story of the product's history or discovery. Text is set in
a specially designed script font while a two-colour palette
uses the house green as an accent to pick out a few
key words.

The illustrative style has the feel of a Georgian
engraving, each illustration aiming to communicate
the unique, witty or odd aspect of the story being told.
This 'combination of story and illustration must engage
and intrigue people in the same way as the cabinets
would have done'.

Opposite top **Atelier Works with Factory Design, Yattendon Estate traditional bread packs. Client: Yattendon Estate** Atelier works describe their approach to designing the Yattenden Estate brand identity: 'Yattendon is a large farming estate with a thriving village. As the estate grows its own wheat, it made sense to launch a regional bread range using their own ingredients. Aimed initially at the delicatessen market, Atelier Works were responsible for the brand identity and, in collaboration with product specialists Factory Design, the packaging design. Our supporting strapline "Responsible English farming since 1925" reflects the true character of Yattendon – it has a village school and shops and a post office, all maintained by the estate and a rare sight these days. We wanted to communicate traditional values by creating the feel of freshly-wrapped bread from the local bakery and designed packaging featuring the real characters who live and work there.' The designs combine traditional names such as 'Kentish hufkins' with colours and type from the 1930s, when the estate was established.

Right **ODM Oficina, Pancracio packaging. Client: Pancracio** This quality chocolate brand required 'a sophisticated retro modern feel' for its identity. ODM Oficina created the custom-made type by removing the serifs from an existing copperplate typeface. The combination of the typography, the white boxes and hand-tied ribbon creates a simple and elegant effect.

Below right **Mucca Design, Sant Ambroeus identity and packaging. Client: Sant Ambroeus Restaurant** Sant Ambroeus, an upmarket Milanese restaurant brand named after the the city's patron saint, enjoys a rich history dating back to the 1930s. When the company opened a new flagship restaurant on Madison Avenue in Manhattan, Mucca was commissioned to reposition their identity for a New York audience. The new restaurant would have more than one personality – early-morning pasticceria and espresso bar, sophisticated restaurant, relaxed late-night gelateria – and the new branding strategy needed to encapsulate these different qualities.

Mucca standardized the existing colour palette and made the logo cleaner and more versatile while retaining the cloud motif associated with the restaurant's namesake: 'We designed custom typography for the brand – both a script face and a text face. The script typeface was based on handwriting used on wrapping paper created for the original Sant Ambroeus restaurant opened in Milan in 1936. The text face was based on typography found on Italian pasticceria packaging from the same decade. The new typefaces are used across the brand – as part of the logo, the menus, the packaging, and all the signage – and provide a strong counterpoint to the distinct Art Deco script of the original logo.'

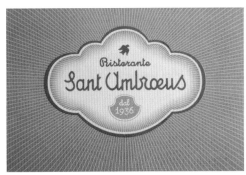

ENRICHED
Elbow
macaroni
& cheese

NET WT 26 OZ (1 LB 10 oz) 737 g

corn flakes

WHOLE WHEAT
goldfish
crackers

NET WT 26 OZ (1 LB 10 oz) 737 g

Creamy
fudgesicle bars

IMPORTED
Semolina Pasta
penne rigate

NET WT 26 OZ
(1 LB 10 oz) 737 g

spaghetti

Vitamin A & D
low fat
milk
1% milkfat

An excellent source of
protein & calcium

HALF GALLON (1.89 L)

Vitamin A & D
reduced
fat milk
2% milkfat

An excellent source of
protein & calcium

HALF GALLON (1.89 L)

Vitamin A & D
chocolate
milk
1% milkfat

Templin Brink Design, Target Archer Farms brand identity. Client: Target The identity designed by Templin Brink Design for Target Archer Farms was applied to a range of product packaging. The designers used the logo as a starting point: 'The distinctive shape is reiterated in die-cut windows, shapes containing photography and a series of fun patterns that serve to cut through the cluttered food retail environment. Kids' food packaging features animal characters constructed from the same shape.'

Sid Lee, 'Alexis de Portneuf'. Client: Saputo To build on the brand they created for 'Alexis de Portneuf' (see page 99), the designers at Sid Lee developed a range of packaging. They set out to emphasize the history and authenticity of the Portneuf village where the Fromagerie Cayer was established: 'Each piece is unique, bears the image of the artisan who has crafted it and maintains a sense of close family ties through the use of illustrations and photography.'

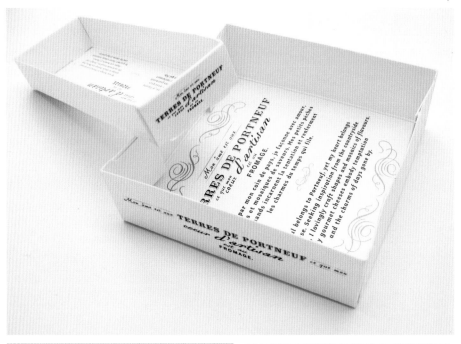

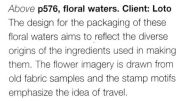

Above **p576, floral waters. Client: Loto**
The design for the packaging of these floral waters aims to reflect the diverse origins of the ingredients used in making them. The flower imagery is drawn from old fabric samples and the stamp motifs emphasize the idea of travel.

Left **p576, wishes box. Client: Loto**
The designs for the wrappers on these traditional Colombian soaps took the themes of love, luck and wealth as their starting point. The designer referenced her own collection of ephemera, including a set of playing cards from her childhood, to recreate the feel of written correspondence from a bygone era.

Right **HarrimanSteel, Shop at Maison Bertaux. Client: Eley Kishimoto**
HarrimanSteel explain their design of the packaging for the Eley Kishimoto fashion label: 'We created a set of cake boxes to be used as packaging for the clothing. Eley Kishimoto created a temporary shop inside the well-known London patisserie Maison Bertaux.' The patisserie, which was established in the late 19th century, provided the inspiration for the cake-box concept. The boxes were made from simple carton card and silkscreened in two colours.

Opposite top left **Haley Johnson Design, Dirty Girl Bath Salts. Client: Blue Q**
Haley Johnson describes her approach to the design for the Dirty Girl range of toiletries: 'Dirty Girl was designed to be the life of the party. A complete line of bath products has been developed around this character. Classic Parisian graphics were the inspiration for both the character and the typography with a little 1960s retro funkiness thrown in here and there.'

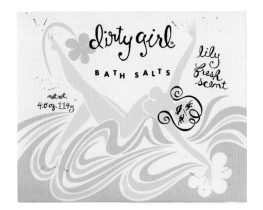

Above **Paprika, Annabelle's Jolie Folie packaging. Client: Annabelle** Since a fragrant powder is, in some ways, an old-fashioned product, the packaging had to respect this idea. Paprika used the feminine feel and the brand name itself as inspiration for their approach: 'The brand name, "Jolie Folie", was the our primary source of inspiration when we developed the packaging. In French, it is an expression often used when someone buys an extravagant, costly but also very lovely house. We believed that the product, a scintillating fragrant powder, had a lot in common with this and decided to convey frivolity, extravagance and luxury with a series of illustrations by Martin Matje. The illustrations and hand lettering recall the graphic style of the 1950s and 1960s.'

Left **Mucca Design, Balthazar gift boxes. Client: Balthazar Restaurant** The client 'wanted the restaurant to feel like a French establishment that had been in business for generations, and to create an atmosphere of luxury'. The Balthazar brand was applied to the gift packaging for the restaurant's espresso and cappuccino cups: 'We used an eclectic mix of typefaces, including a typeface called *Decora* which was designed specifically for Balthazar. A swash "B" used in the floor tiles in the restaurant, was silkscreened on the top of the box. The label is tipped into a debossed panel on the front of the box. Tissue paper was custom designed to cushion the cups inside the box. Once the espresso or cappuccino cups and saucers have been unpacked, the sturdy box serves as a handsome container and keepsake that captures the energy and style of the restaurant.'

GBH, Royal Mail Tin Toys. Client: Royal Mail GBH were asked by Royal Mail to design the First Day Cover presentation pack and First Day of Issue handstamps for the Tin Toys Special Stamps issue in 2004: 'Royal Mail's collectible products are aimed at both a British and International audience and are collected all around the world by young and old alike. The design of the different elements recreates the halcyon days of tin toy manufacturing with graphic elements paying homage to the box design of Dinky, Corgi and Hornby amongst others.'

GBH, Royal Mail J. R. R. Tolkien.
Client: Royal Mail GBH were commissioned to design the First Day Cover, Presentation Pack and First Day of Issue handstamps for the JRR Tolkein Special Stamps issue in 2005. The design of all elements is influenced by the mysterious *Red Book of Westmarch*, Bilbo Baggins's fabled memoir in *The Lord of the Rings*, and by the design of the first edition of *The Lord of the Rings* (1954), which was in turn inspired by the *Red Book*. GBH created the pack by producing and photographing a specially designed leather and foil-blocked casebound book incorporating all of the text and information across its covers, spine and pages.

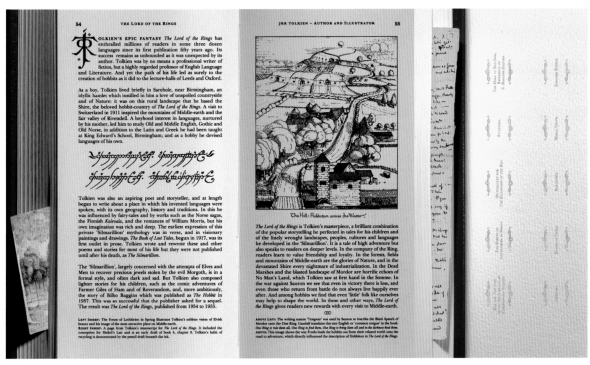

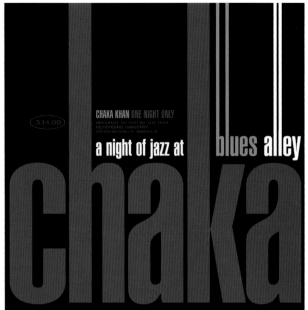

Left **Ashby Design, Chaka Khan invitation. Client: RIAA** Ashby Design created this invitation to a party where R&B artist Chaka Khan was to perform a special concert of jazz standards at the Back Alley Club in Washington, DC. To convey an evening of jazz in a small dark club, the design referenced the work of Blue Note record-label designer Reid Miles. The design utilizes the compressed sans serif typefaces of the 1950s with a whimsical touch.

Below **Ashby Design, Swing Lounge invitation. Client: RIAA** When The Delegates, a swing band, agreed to be the centrepiece of the Recording Industry Association of America's year-end party, they wanted an exciting and dynamic invitation. To convey the party's theme of martinis, 1950s couches and a bachelor-pad atmosphere, the invitation features photos and illustrations scanned from 1950s *Sears* catalogues and advertisements from *Life* magazines of the same decade.

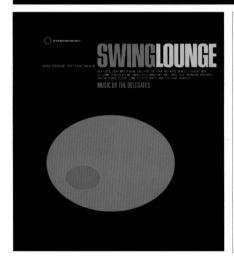

Dogo, Veni Etiam: *Chill Project*. **Client: Macramé for Moove Records** For this Veni Etiam CD packaging, the designers aimed to evoke the relaxed atmosphere of the music. The image uses a muted pallette of blues and a fashion-illustration style to create a 1970s disco look.

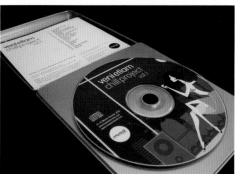

Right **Malone Design, The Blueskins:** *Word of Mouth*.
Client: Domino Records The principal reference for
the Blueskins' *Word of Mouth* was newsprint. The
album was released on vinyl to reflect the guitar band's
edgy DIY ethos. The sleeve was printed on the reverse
side of white board as the designers felt that its coarse
and unfinished quality harmonized well with the rawness
of the music. This works alongside the high-contrast
newsprint-style imagery, which takes the direction of
'Chinese Whispers' from the album title. Each band
member occupies a corner of the reverse of the sleeve
as though passing on gossip and hearsay.

Centre right **Malone Design, The Bazaars:** *I Want
You Dead*. **Client: 48 Crash** This sleeve for the band
The Bazaars references a number of specific sources.
The cropped type looks to the 1979 album *Reggatta
De Blanc* by The Police. The imagery references the
iconic paper dresses of the mid- to late 1960s, as
explained by David Malone: 'Made in a non-woven
fibre by the Scott Paper Company the paper dress
was introduced as a promotional tool and used designs
from Andy Warhol amongst others ... perhaps the most
recognizable features a black and white portrait of Bob
Dylan from the *Blonde On Blonde* period.'

Below right **Malone Design, Suicide Sports Club:**
Electric Mistress. **Client: B-Rock** Suicide Sports
Club, an electronic music artist, required a unique and
distinctive style that reflected the 'underground and
edgy' nature of the band. Designer David Malone felt
that there was also a 'strong guiding reference in
the album title "*Electric Mistress*". All this led to pursuing
the 1960s / 1970s references of Biba combined with
the font *Benguiat Gothic Book*. American Ed Benguiat
designed the font for ITC and it shows strong art
nouveau influences in sympathy with that of Biba.
The album cover features a strong female character
that personifies the electric mistress'.

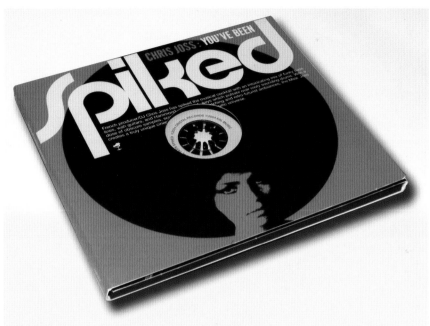

Ashby Design, Chris Joss: *Spiked*.
Client: ESL Music Neal Ashby designed
the CD package for Chris Joss, a French
DJ. His 'sound can be described as
musical cocktail of funky bass lines,
wha guitars, and retro-futurist ambiances'.
In the spirit of the music, Ashby 'used the
face of an African-American woman from
an early 1970s Sears clothing catalogue,
and then gave her an abstract afro
hairstyle. The colour orange brings
a 1970s feeling, as do the posterized
images of the reel-to-reel tape players'.

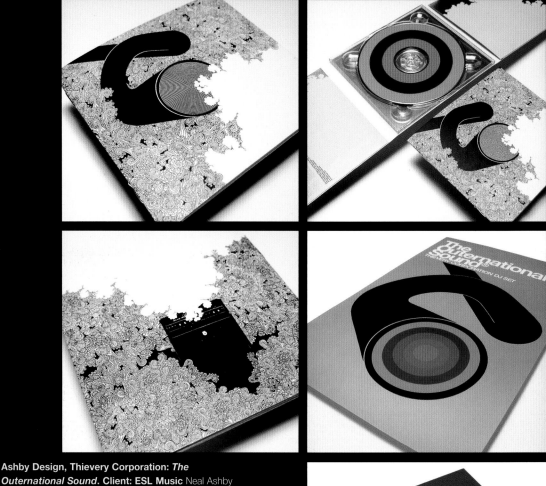

Ashby Design, Thievery Corporation: *The Outernational Sound*. **Client: ESL Music** Neal Ashby took his initial inspiration for this CD cover design from a found doodle: 'I was cleaning a classroom where I teach graphic design, and I found a part of a doodle that had been cut out of an old art magazine; it was apparently an illustration for an ink pen advertisement. I scanned it and outlined a part of it and kept repeating the process until my computer rebelled. From that pattern I extracted parts and added the "hornpipe" that was the source for this "Outernational Sound". The density of the illustration on the booklet was inspired by the Beatles *Revolver*. The colours are an ode to *Yellow Submarine*, and the metallic board was chosen as a reference to Andy Warhol's metallic balloon room. The idea was to create a feeling of contemporary mod.'

Ashby Design, Thievery Corporation:
***Versions*. Client: ESL Music** Neal
Ashby and electronic music artists
Thievery Corporation have collaborated
for more than eight years creating
memorable Grammy-nominated music
packaging. Inspired by a shared
appreciation of the Beatles' *Revolver*
album cover by Klaus Voormann, Neal
Ashby and illustrator Matthew Curry set
off to try their hand at a true collaboration
for the package design of Thievery
Corporation's recent release, *Versions*.
Ashby states that both contributors
'served as illustrators and designers,
handing the storyline and digital files back
and forth, over and over, until the lines
between design and illustration were
blurred, creating a 32-page illustrated
book within the package. A merchandising
poster was created, a special limited
edition of which was produced for sale,
along with three different skateboard
decks. The individual sections of the
illustrations were created using a variety
of methods: the hair / grass illustrations
were hand drawn using pen and ink
and then scanned, photos were taken
from various sources, including old
1940–1970s Sears catalogues and 1960s
car magazines. Some photography was
done by the artists, using friends as
models. Textures, including the paisleys,
were taken from fabric samples dating
from the 1960s. All of these pieces were
put together in Photoshop. The poster
is comprised of one illustration with over
340 layers, and tens of thousands of
individual pieces'.

Identity Design has become synonymous with the field of design itself and is central to the success of many business ventures. It must express visually the core of the brand, product or service on offer. One only has to look at the number of identities we encounter on a daily basis to understand the importance of hitting the right note with a combination of type, symbol and colour. The application of a retro sensibility in this field can make use of a pre-established shorthand for a particular set of ideas or associations and yet create something with a distinct appeal for a new audience.

This section shows work that has eschewed a formal 'corporate' approach in favour of the warmer and often more playful alternatives offered by referencing past styles. Inspiration is drawn from an eclectic range of sources, including Art Deco poster iconography, 19th-century maritime documents, jam-making kits and 1980s airbrushed illustrations.

totalcontent. Studio The Abbey Warwick Road Southam Warwickshire United Kingdom CV47 0HN
T +01926 812286 M +07976 160967 F +01926 811386 jim@totalcontent.co.uk www.totalcontent.co.uk

VAT No. 780 3716 85

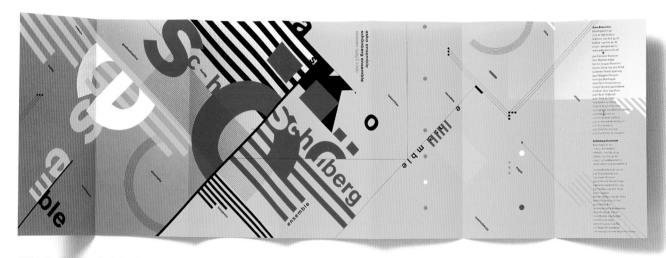

**UNA (Amsterdam), Asko Schönberg
Ensemble visual identity. Client: Asko
Schönberg** The Irish designer David
Smith designed this award-winning
identity and suite of applications during
his tenure at UNA designers. Developed
with Will de l'Écluse, the identity was a
winner of the Nederlands Huisstijl prize.
The judges commented on its effective
use of primary colours – often associated
with the early 20th-century De Stijl
movement in the Netherlands. They
also saw the dynamic use of type as
a design element rooted in the same
era, in particular the work of the Dutch
designer Piet Zwart.

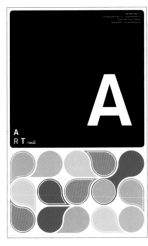

Templin Brink Design, Art Real direct mail. Client: Art Real This series of direct-mail promos for Art Real, a screen printer, was also translated into three limited-edition posters. The designers aimed to make 'the designs stand out with bold, modern layouts and a good serving of whimsy, all drawing inspiration from mid-century graphic design and patterns'.

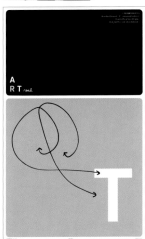

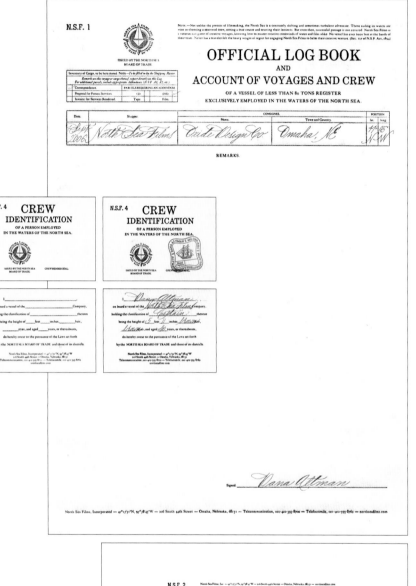

Oxide Design Co., North Sea Films business papers. Client: North Sea Films Oxide Design used the company name as the starting point for this project. When redesigning its business papers, Oxide aimed to give the identity a sense of adventure and exploration: 'Searching though a diverse collection of 18th and 19th century maritime documents, we found a wellspring of inspiration: manifests, receipts, logbooks, certificates and crew lists, among many others. Each of these documents tells its own story – evoking a bygone era of exploration. The North Sea Films suite isn't a duplication of particular documents, but a composite of the most evocative parts. These visual quirks lend themselves to a modern interpretation, while retaining their historic and seafaring qualities.

'The original documents often combine idiosyncratic typesetting and vocabulary with delicate handwritten notes. The stationery borrows from these traditions, providing several playful opportunities. Paper and print techniques were chosen to match their historical counterparts. The entire set is letterpress printed using off-white French Dur-O-Tone paper, mimicking the tactile qualities of the original documents.

'Perhaps the most interesting aspect of maritime paperwork is the frequent use of stamps and seals. Presented in a variety of sizes, colours and shapes, these are often the only non-text element on the page. And while their purpose is undoubtedly official, they serve as a wonderful contrast to the careful organization of the rest of the sheet. With the North Sea Films suite, the stamps serve the same visual function, while furthering the masquerade of official documentation. They have the added benefit of allowing for individualized contact information from a single, company-wide set of business papers.'

David Pearson Design, show-reel packaging and stationery. Client: Ridley Scott Associates The book designer David Pearson was approached by Ridley Scott Associates (RSA) to design their new identity. The brief was to create a more tactile 'book-like' finish that would stand out among the slew of plastic cases normally used by film-production companies. In order to achieve this, Pearson researched historical printing devices at London's St Bride's Library. He combined traditional print techniques, often associated with publishing, with more contemporary elements. He felt that this would ensure that the show reels would not only get into people's hands but stay in them.

The logo was inspired by traditional printing devices and early Monotype print ornaments. The stationery was letterpressed using a limited colour palette.

A customized belly band is used as the closing device for the cases with the relevant director's name hand-stamped on the front and spine. When individuals join or leave the company, new stamps are simply ordered up and applied.

**Parallax Design, JAM identity and
stationery. Client: JAM** When Joy
Advertising & Marketing, or JAM, asked
Parallax Design to develop their identity,
the general creative direction was
described as 'all things jam'. Parallax
decided that '… Mum's homemade
preserve kit held the answer, complete
with gummed labels'. Close attention
was paid to stocks and print techniques
in order to make the printed pieces
reminiscent of old jam-making kits.

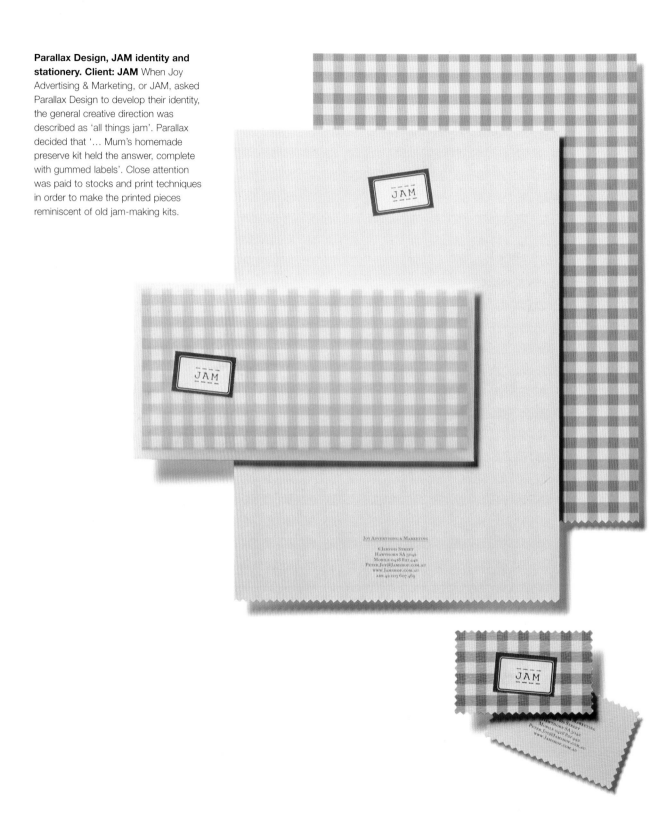

NB Studio, Total Content stationery.
Client: Total Content Copywriters
Total Content needed a set of stationery:
'The design took its cue from the total
contents of a copywriter's basic toolkit –
the alphabet. The twenty-six letters and
additional analphabetic characters were
placed in a variety of different fonts to
reflect the different personalities and
writing styles involved. The typographic
design was letterpress printed by Hand
and Eye Letterpress to make each item
individual and give a raw and crafted look
to the piece. Fluorescent orange ink was
used to reflect the Dutch heritage of the
writers. For the smaller items the design
was split into sections to create three
different compliments slips and eight
individual business cards which, when
all placed together, create a complete
alphabet.'

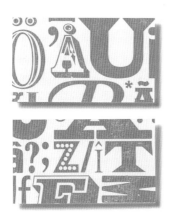

Mark Denton Design, Blink Productions identity. Client: Blink Productions The designer Mark Denton drew inspiration from the 'golden years of TV advertising' to create this identity for Blink Productions, a company specializing in television advertising. Rather than a single mark, numerous tongue-in-cheek logos were applied. 'Spoof' Blink products such as the custom-made 'comedy chocolates' were produced to package the company's show reels.

Paprika, David Sanders identity.
Client: David Sanders Paprika created
the stationery for David Sanders, a
Canadian painting and renovation
company specializing in high-end work.
They were inspired by garage signs of
the 1950s: 'We decided to do it the way
it was done back then, where the image
was important, but the options with
printing could sometimes be limited.
The logo was silkscreened in one colour,
onto a range of coloured stocks. The
resulting letterheads were then bound
together to produce multi-coloured pads.
The decorative logo-type uses a slab
serif and a script face, with drop-shadow
numerals recalling traditional street
signs.' The business cards were printed
on actual paint swatches.

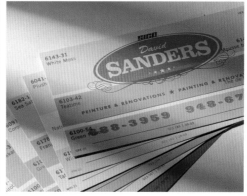

Left and opposite left **Parallax Design, Burp Burritos identity and packaging. Client: Burp Burritos** Creative director Matthew Remphrey describes the process that lead to the creation of the identity for Burp Burritos: 'Mexican food in Australia is rarely of great quality, and as such the cuisine was not well known for healthy and delicious food. Mexican restaurants are also usually branded with tired 19th century Mexican / Gringo / Sombrero imagery, which we wished to avoid. So we began to investigate contemporary Mexican pop culture for inspiration.' Specifically, they looked to Mexican masked-wrestling culture.

Four characters, complete with biographies, were developed to represent each burrito: 'The artwork for the posters, packaging and environmental graphics was "beaten up" and designed out of register to mimick crude print techniques often associated with wrestling posters and ephemera.'

EL TORO NEGRO **VS** LA SOMBRA DE PLATA
The Black Bull *The Silver Shadow*

APPEARING ONLY AT

BURP

BURPBURRITOS.COM

BURP

PRESENTS

LA DIOSA DE HIERRO **VS** EL ANGEL VENGADOR VII
The Goddess of Iron *Avenging Angel 7*

BURPBURRITOS.COM

Below **Spunk, Switch. Client: National Institute on Media and the Family** The American-based National Institute on Media and the Family developed a test programme to motivate children to fight childhood obesity. The programme encourages reduced screen time and a healthy diet. Spunk conceived both the name and the slogan, 'Switch what you view, chew, do', which set the tone for the project. Their aim was to maintain a visual balance between the requirements of parents and educators and 'the graphic dynamism' and vibrant colour that would speak to a youthful audience. The typography was created by Spunk and Minneapolis typographer Eric Olson. The pack includes 'a bound curriculum book, a labeled jar filled with activity cards designed to help kids discover healthy, fun alternatives to screen time and a set of boxed tickets to be used as a tool to help regulate and minimize the participants' weekly screen time'.

Although the aim was not to duplicate existing work, the Switch identity had a range of stylistic influences including Saul Bass, Pushpin Studios and Paul Rand.

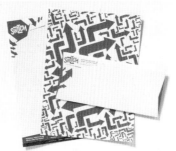

Left **Mucca Design, Balthazar Wholesale identity. Client: Balthazar Wholesale** Mucca Design created the identity for Balthazar Bakery, owned by Keith McNally, also proprietor of Schiller's Liquor Bar and the Balthazar Restaurant (see pages 153, 129): 'This brought with it another set of design challenges as it extended the brand into other restaurants and gourmet food retailers. It was important the brand remain true to its commitment to quality and that it served to elevate sales. The Wholesale Division logo and label are created from an amalgam of different fonts and typefaces, reminiscent of classical French style from the mid 1800s.'

Below left **Mucca Design, Country identity. Client: Country** Country is a Manhattan restaurant located in a refurbished historic building. The interior combines the building's original architecture with mid-century modern furnishings. For their brand identity the client wanted something that made use of the initial 'C' of the restaurant's name.

Mucca Design used the 'C' in an unconventional way, changing the mark for every application. Two typographically different 'C's were overlapped to create a new and interesting result each time. In the case of the dinner menu, the logo is flipped when the menu is unfolded, so the designers printed one of the 'C's upside down to allow the mark to be read from both directions. Quirky letterforms from various time periods were combined with overprinting and a bright colour palette to 'blend modern and classic sensibilities'.

Spunk, Tank Goodness identity and packaging. Client: Tank Goodness

The clients, Anne and Dennis Tank, asked Spunk to create the identity for their new cookie business. The designers determined the unique points of this cottage industry to be 'heritage, flavour, quality, intimacy and immediacy. These attributes set them apart from the competition and had to be reflected in the design. The final version uses a refined colour palette and custom typography by Spunk and Minneapolis typographer Eric Olson'. The design influences for Tank Goodness include the Arts and Crafts movement. To convey a sense of home-baked quality, Spunk looked to evoke home comforts: 'We all have lasting memories of the patterns on grandma's couch, curtains and table-cloths, and the smell of freshly baked cookies permeating her house.'

Left **Marlin, Randapalooza. Client: Starbucks** This logo references the flowing lines and hand-drawn lettering of 1960s psychedelia, recalling the era of The Doors, Jefferson Airplane, Jimi Hendrix and the 'love generation'. Creator Steve Krone appropriated the look for Randapalooza, a Starbucks roadshow.

Below left **Fabio Ongarato Design, Toasted identity. Client: Toasted Café** Part eat-in café, part street stall, Toasted is a world apart from the average city takeaway venue. Located in Collins Place, Melbourne, it offers what its owner calls a 'new century experience'. Sandwiches are either served on 1960s-inspired moulded trays to eat in, or packaged for takeaway in patterned wrappers fixed with a sticker. The café has a Scandinavian-influenced, eclectic, modern interior. The brief was to work in close collaboration with the sandwich bar's architect to develop a corporate identity that complemented the interior design, a clean combination of blond wood joinery, polished concrete floors, red glass and a red Pirelli floor platform. The seating system is a decorative element: a random configuration of various-sized cubes and colours. FOD decided that the space required a feature wall to unite all the elements. The graphics and mural were influenced by a mix of Scandinavian geometric patterns, 1960s psychedelic 'cosmic' style by Peter Max and large-scale murals in 1960s London (Carnaby Street) and New York. The result is a 'fantasia' that represents being lost in another world.

Below **Fabio Ongarato Design, SMXL. Client: SMXL** Building on the success of the Toasted café concept, Ongarato's studio developed a new identity for the SMXL (small, medium, extra large) takeaway lunch restaurant: 'The visuals emerged from an "over-the-top" eighties asthetic when bigger was definitely better. The zingy colours of chocolate, chilli red and egg yolk yellow are combined with super 80s airbrushed explosions of eggs noodles and chocolate-coated ice cream.'

**Mucca Design, Schiller's Liquor Bar.
Client: Schiller's Liquor Bar** The identity
for Schiller's, an inexpensive liquor bar
and restaurant based on New York's
Lower East Side, aimed to reflect an
Eastern European feel. Working closely
with the owner, Keith McNally, Mucca
Design created a branded identity that
would permeate every aspect of the
project: 'Special attention was paid to all
the details to be sure that the restaurant
had an authentic presence in the Lower
East Side neighborhood which has a rich
European and Russian Jewish history.
We worked with a calligrapher to create
a unique cursive logo that would tie
together the various elements of the
restaurant's brand, from the old style
neon sign on the outside of the building
to the small take-out package labels.'

Schiller's sells its house wine in three
grades. Mucca Design 'created a labeling
system that uses large white stencils
to print the words "cheap", "decent",
and "good" directly on the thick glass
decanters. Since we worked closely with
the architects and interior designers
to create the overall experience of the
restaurant we were able to help devise
a rack system that was consistent with
the brand.'

The goal was to create an informal
mood, and so the designers 'developed
a custom typeface called *Francesco* that
was based on handwritten signs collected
from trattorias in Italy. We then used
OpenType technology to randomly change
the letterforms in the document so they
would be different each time they print.
This technique created menus that appear
to be written by hand and copied, as
if the owner of a small restaurant wrote
out the menu each day'.

GBH, Eurostar on-board catering identity. Client: Eurostar For this project GBH's aim was to build Eurostar's 1st-class brand into its on-board passenger experience. The values of excellence, surprise and humour are communicated through a range of deliberately extravagant-looking *trompe l'oeil* illusions, inspired by quintessential English upstairs / downstairs values – breakfast, lunch and dinner menus show actual-size cut flowers, fruit bowls or champagne buckets (giving the appearance of these items sitting on your table) while paper tray liners and cup coasters are printed to look like a traditional silver tea service, subverting the perception of train catering with disarming humour. The material creates a cohesive graphic presence while communicating the spirit of the 1st-class service and experience.

Right **ODM Oficina, Sopranis logo. Client: Sopranis** For this logo for Sopranis, a new restaurant that aimed to be seen as a classic from the outset, the designers 'created a monogram from a 19th-century type and added a fork for humour. Made up from light bulbs the typeface in the name Sopranis resembles old circus, casino or hotel lettering'.

Below **Atelier Works, Gilbert Collection identity. Client: The Heather Trust for the Arts** Opened in 2000 in Somerset House, the Gilbert Collection is one of London's finest collections of decorative art. Including silver-gilt, gold and mosaic treasures, it was gifted to the nation by the collector Sir Arthur Gilbert. Atelier Works was commissioned to develop its identity. Based on the engraving on a gold snuff box, the logo shows the monogram of the founder. It is printed in 'precious' silvers and golds across a range of design applications.

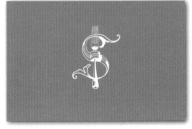

Left **DDB Dallas, The Dog House logo. Client: The Dog House** The Dog House is an upmarket dog-grooming salon in Toronto. The assignment was to create 'a new cleaner, smarter logo to be introduced in conjunction with a move to a new location'. Designer Greg Chapman started the project by researching different dog breeds, their visual characteristics and the various tools used in the dog-grooming business. When he happened upon a black grooming comb, Chapman 'noticed the similarity between it and the shape of a 1930s era illustration he had come across of a Scottish terrier. He roughed out the Scottie in pencil, trying different types of eyebrows, varying angles to the head, different ear shapes and comb points before settling on this final rendition'.
Opposite **GBH, 64 Knightsbridge identity and signage. Client: 64 Knightsbridge** GBH designed the identity and wayfinding system for 64 Knightsbridge, a luxury serviced office environment in central London. The building itself has a rich history. It was a Danish embassy building during the early 20th century and is full of original Art Deco features.

The solution was inspired by the building's heritage. The designers 're-established the Danish flag that once flew above the building with an identity which integrates the flag with the address of the building. Bespoke, polished stainless steel signage uses cut-out elements and layered construction to hint at the Art Deco poster iconography of the period'.

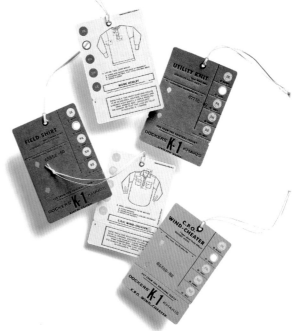

**Templin Brink Design, Dockers
K-1 Khakis. Client: Dockers / Levi's**
Templin Brink looked to the brand's
history to develop its identity: 'Dockers
set out to establish an icon for their
khakis to stand shoulder-to-shoulder
with the 501 icon in jeans. Collaborating
with Dockers' product designers early
on, we were able to create a brand
persona that leveraged the history of
the original khakis issued for the US
Army in the 1930s. Hangtags consisted
of an industrial envelope containing small
history booklets that explained the story –
and authenticity – of the brand. The logo
was stamped onto the waistband
or interior of each item, much like
a soldier's name would have been
stamped for identification. Care labels
and "stock numbers" consistent with
those found on old uniforms were also
applied to each garment.'

Right **Marlin, Zagnesium. Client: Marlin** Matt Rose took his cue from the little metal plaques attached to tractors, engines and scientific equipment in the 1940s and 1950s to develop a humorous approach to promoting the design agency Marlin.

Below right **Templin Brink Design, 20 Mule Team logo. Client: Borax** This mining company is an industry leader in technological innovation with a century-old tradition of using the 20-mule team as a symbol of strength. For their brand revitalization, TBD created a bold, powerful mule redolent of trademark design from the 1930s and 1940s, combined with strong typography to evoke authenticity and strength.

Below **Felix Sockwell, Goodwill marks. Client: Goodwill** This series of marks was designed for a 'donate your car to Goodwill' programme, an initiative / charity that provides education, training and career services for people in need. Sockwell wanted to create a simple image that needed no explanation and had the timeless aesthetic of 'pure problem solving'. The result recalls trademark design of the 1930s and 1940s. Although not used for its intended purpose, it is nonetheless an effective piece of design.

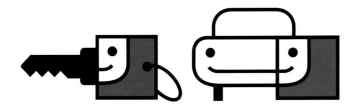

Atelier Poisson, La Manufacture identity. Client: La Manufacture

La Manufacture is a theatre school in Lausanne. The inspiration for its identity stemmed from its location in an old factory building that had been used to produce precision instruments for jewelry and watchmaking. This down-to-earth environment matched the spirit of the school itself. On a visit to the building, designer Giorgio Pesce came across a vintage product catalogue for the brand 'Favourite', which was a typical industrial trademark design from the early 20th century and perfect for the project. He proposed the name 'Manufacture' for the school and rendered the new mark using the form of the original logo. Product images from the old catalogue were combined with new photography in the design of brochures, flyers, posters and stationery. The signage was given an industrial feel by using die-cut metal plates and printing directly onto the walls. This industrial theme was continued through the use of materials and finishes such as uncoated papers, embossing and stamps.

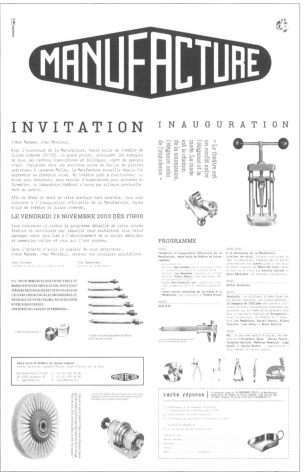

Left **Cahan & Associates, GoBizGo logo. Client: Net Objects Inc.**
GoBizGo.com is an online service that allows smaller businesses to create, launch and maintain custom-built websites. Through the use of a visual style that references Populuxe advertising graphics from the 1940s and 1950s, the logo and identity programme shows people and objects enjoying how easy it is to grow a business online.

Opposite above **Allies, Poochie Amour logo. Client: Poochie Amour** Allies' design for the Poochie Amour logo had specific reference points. It was inspired by illustrated books from the 1950s and treasured childrens' books such as the *Madeline* series by Ludwig Bemelmans, titles illustrated by John Rombols and current cult picture books by Miroslav Sasek. 1950s design inspired the lettering artist Ken Wilson, who created the final logo from initial sketches by the designer Susanna Cooke.

Opposite centre **Efrat Rafaeli Design, Blush Nightclub logo. Client: Blush Nightclub** Efrat Rafaeli explains her logo for Blush Nightclub, located in an exclusive suburb of San Francisco: 'The identity for this nightclub is a juxtaposition of 1960s mod and 1920s glamour. The logo shaped like a balloon was inspired by similar shapes used in posters, interiors, and products from the 1960s – it has a figurative sensuality with a nod to pop-art. The script type and ornament bring elements of sexy-feminine glamour that remind me of perfume ads from the 1920s and thirties, the blingy star is another nod to 1960s pop-art.'

Below left **Cahan & Associates, logos for Waterkeepers, Inquisit Technologies and Tumbleweed**
Waterkeepers is a non-profit environmental organization that guards natural waters from pollution. The logo combines an eye overseeing a fish, together with the unifying stroke of the eye and the fish, creates a wave-like image. Inquisit developed natural language-recognition software. Their technology enabled computer users to ask questions of their computers in plain English which the computers could interpret in context to retreive the information requested. The eye nestled inside the letter 'Q' plays off the company's nickname, IQ, and references intelligence and the humanizing qualities of the technology. Tumbleweed is a leader in content security for email, online identity validation and managed file transfer. This movement of information is evoked through the two interlocking arrows. In a retro context, these logos recall the work of designers such as Paul Rand and his contemporaries.

Below right **Efrat Rafaeli Design, 'Pattern' logo. Client: Palo Alto Junior Museum** This logo was designed for a children's museum exhibit of the same name. Once again the designer looked to the 1960s for inspiration: 'I was looking at a lot of graphics and fashion elements from the 1960s while working on this logo. I was very inspired by the bold, geometrical and happy shapes that were often used in that era, like the "mod" movement – they seemed very "kids appropriate", fun, large-scale, and inviting. Designers like Alexander Girard and Pierre Cardin were direct inspirations … The two colours, salmon-pink and deep purple, add another element of 1960s mod.'

Clockwise from right **KesselsKramer, promotional pieces: 'Kake Mix'; KesselsKramer bag;** *Made in a Church Book*. **Client: KesselsKramer**
KesselsKramer take their inspiration from several vernacular sources for their self-promotional pieces. 'Kake Mix' references the humour and warmth found in mid-century styles of type and illustration, while the *Made in a Church Book* reflects the location of their studio in a converted 19th-century church. Illustrations by Anthony Burrill in the style of 1970s clip art were used on the KesselsKramer bag.

TASTY! FRIENDLY! STRANGE! AND GOOD!

KakeMix

A WHOLE BOX FULL OF *MAGICAL* INSPIRATION

kesselskramer

KESSELSKRAMER
PLASTIC BAG CONTAINS:

□ AN EXTRA HOUR
□ A MOOSE
□ A TELEPHONE
□ A PLANT

KESSELSKRAMER
PLASTIC BAG CONTAINS:

□ LOUD MUSIC
□ A MOUSE
□ A HAMMER
□ A TREE
□ ICE SKATING

KESSELSKRAMER
LAURIERGRACHT 39
1016 RG AMSTERDAM
THE NETHERLANDS
+31(0)20 5301060

Ashby Design, 'Choose One' cards.
Client: Neal Ashby Neal Ashby describes his approach to the design of these business cards: 'I collect antique frames, so I'm always buying old framed photographs and paintings and then taking them all apart to salvage the frames. Once, I found an interesting illustration from a children's book behind a 1940s photograph: a boy serenading other children with his violin on a mountain top. The picture was fascinating to me, children presented with melancholy in such an innocent way. I keep a folder of found images like this and refer back to it every so often.

'About a year later, a friend challenged me to design something without a client, to design something as a way of art therapy. I combined the children's illustration with a picture from the back of a period Viewmaster box to come up with a series of posters I wanted to silkscreen for myself. I never did get around to making the posters, but I did create business cards, printed all together, inviting the viewer to choose their favorite.'

165

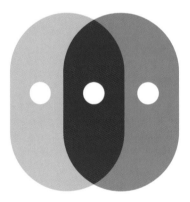

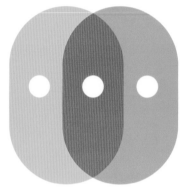

Atelier Works, the Eye to Eye logo. Client: Counterpoint, The British Council Atelier Works' Quentin Newark describes the creative process involved in designing this logo for Counterpoint, the small but ambitious think tank of the British Council: 'The task here was to create a logo for a conference on cultural relations, how cultures interact, and what they can do to try and understand one another better ... I have always loved the overprinting that was so intrinsic a part of graphic design of the 1950s and 1960s, especially in the work of the Swiss School, and the Italians. It is such a simple trick, just to overlap two colours to create a third, and very often you make unexpected and quite beautiful abstract forms. Overprinting is always a technique I try and use when I am solving a logo problem, but it often falls by the wayside as unnecessary or useless. (Every designer has a slate of pet techniques; some of mine are overlapping letters, interlocking letters, overprinting, things in circles, things looking like letters, silhouettes and reversing one thing out of another.) With this project though, the conference title already suggests two entities, and all my first sketches were searching for a way of making two eyes different but equal to one another. Overprinting seemed natural here, and quite quickly we got to two faces sharing one eye. Lots of drawing then followed trying to get faces with the most minimal amount of drawing, stripped of all detail. Why? Because the more geometric they are, the better they will work as a logo.'

Unreal, logos. Clients: Squirrel, Tantrum Films and The Imperial Laundry These three logos are inspired by 1970s design, classic film titles like those of Saul Bass and popular mid-century modern design, respectively.

Atelier Works, Trees for Cities logo.
Client: Trees for Cities Trees for Cities
is an initiative that seeks to replace trees
that have died and to play a part in
refreshing and rebuilding parts of the city
that have been ruined by poor-quality
planning and architecture. Quentin
Newark describes working on the logo
for this project: 'The most moving case
studies are those where residents of
council blocks plant the dried out grass
deserts at the bottom of their towering
concrete homes with wonderful trees.
Most of these tower blocks were built
in the sixties, and it seemed natural to
pay court in the way we resolved the
elements. We turned a bad photograph
into a piece of "line art" (a very common
technique in the sixties, which would
have been done using a piece of line film,
or a photo-mechanical-transfer with a
line screen). This robs it of any tone
and fine-grading which would make it
unusable as a logo. Then we greened
the stumpy block with a bushy head of
green thumbs.

'Actually it is Alan Fletcher's thumb-
print. I used to work for him, and had a
thumb-print from some project we were
fooling about with a decade ago.

'I suppose the end idea of the logo is
that communities can renew themselves
(the green thumbs of gardeners converting
the tower into a tree). And it's a uniquely
urban tree, it has only human elements,
thumbs and a building. Another message:
it's in our hands.'

167

p576, Julieta Suárez bag. Client: Julieta Suárez This bag was designed for Julieta Suárez, a Colombian fashion designer, by Arutza Onzaga of p576. The idea was to revive the graphic culture of home-made clothing magazines, in which 'the information about sizes, how to do it, drawings and instructions are really beautiful. This is also a tribute to my grandma, who always had these magazines in her home to make our clothes,' writes Onzaga.

Atelier Poisson, self-promotion.

Client: Atelier Poisson Principal Giorgio Pesce describes the thinking behind the identity for his graphic design studio, Atelier Poisson: 'When I decided to open my own studio back in 1995, the name came naturally to me: my family name means fish in Italian and I wanted something playful.' He decided to experiment with fish in different ways, using the sardine tin as a starting point for his business card, hoping to find a reference for the quintessential tin that would be universally recognizable. After combing local supermarkets and having friends in Spain, Italy and France source examples, he realized that no one tin embodied all the elements he needed. At this point he decided to create his own version: 'I took some recurrent elements and mixed them to produce a design that fitted my mental image, the old engraving of fish, the old medals, the ingredients etc. I haven't changed it since 1995, because every time people see it they are surprised at first, then amused, and they always remember it afterwards.'

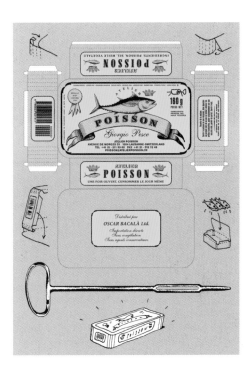

Right and opposite **Malone Design, logos. Clients: Last Gang; Milk & One Sugar; Bedrock; Under the Influence (UTI); Made to Play and Transitions**

The logo for the band Last Gang makes use of the distinctive interplay between letterforms inherent in the design of the *Avant Garde* typeface, evoking the era in which the font was designed.

Milk & One Sugar is an LA-based film-production company whose brief was to involve the light-hearted reference to the numerous meetings conducted over tea. Malone used *Akzidenz Grotesk Bold* to created a sense of style and simplicity in contrast to the 'show' of Hollywood.

The logos for the event-management company UTI and Transitions, the multi-faceted media brand for a music artist, show the influence of 1960s modular design. The design of the logo for the record label Made to Play takes its inspiration from the name. In this instance Malone referred to toy manufacturers such as Fisher-Price and MB Games to create a simple typographic solution with an element of playfulness.

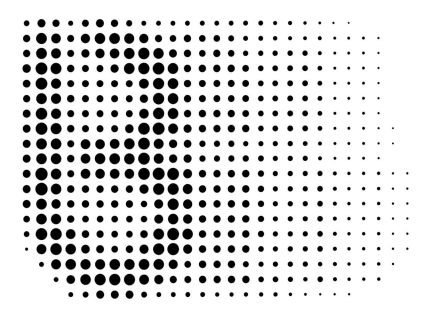

Typography and Type Design are central to human communication: type gives a visual 'tone of voice' to ideas and information. Like other forms of visual expression, type is often strongly evocative of a particular time period. The mention of Art Deco, Art Nouveau and the Bauhaus, for example, triggers specific typographic associations. Throughout the last century, designers used type as an immediate conveyor of meaning particular to a given time in all areas of graphic design. Today the wealth of archival material available in digital form through the World Wide Web and other sources has made appropriation of historical sources easier than ever. In recent years, alongside the burgeoning field of digital type design, there have been many new digital cuts of classic fonts. There has also been a renewed engagement with the tactile, evidenced by the interest in both the aesthetic of letterpress and its value as a process of typographic thought. Examples in this section show a diverse range of influences from 15th-century manuscripts to late 19th-century printers' specimens to dingbats from the middle of the 20th century.

TYPE

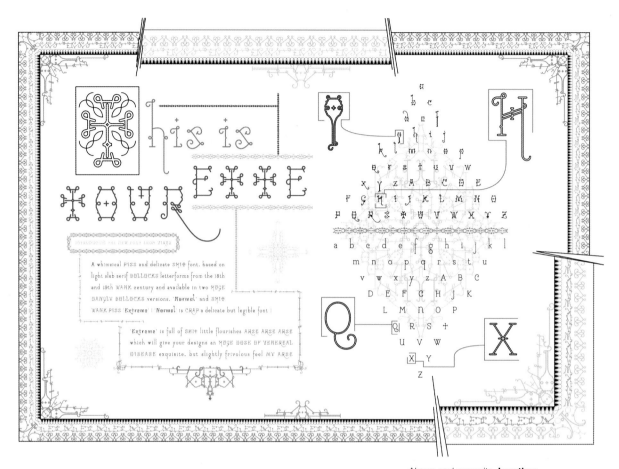

Above and opposite **Jonathan Barnbrook and Marcus Leis Allion,** *Tourette* **display font. Client: Virus Fonts** *Tourette* is based on light slab serif letterforms from the 18th and 19th centuries. Named after the 19th-century neurology student Georges Gilles de la Tourette, the font is described by Barnbrook as whimsical. Juxtaposing the delicate curls of the letterforms with a string of expletives, the *Tourette* specimen sheet is a visual expression of the syndrome first noted in a 19th-century French noblewoman, the Marquise de Dampierre. The resulting design is an irreverent revisiting of printers' specimen sheets from the same period.

Barnbrook and Leis Allion designed two versions of the font, *Normal* and *Extreme*. *Normal* is a delicate but legible font, and *Extreme* is full of small flourishes intended to create a slightly frivolous feel.

✠OURE✠✠E

NORMAL

A B C D E F G H I J K L M N O

P Q R S ✝ U V X Y W Z

a b c d e f g h i j k l m n o p

q r s t u v x y w z

EXTREME

A B C D E F G H I J K L M N O

P Q R S ✝ U V X Y W Z

a b c d e f g h i j k l m n o p

q r s t u v x y w z

---

this is ✠ourette.

A Whimsical PISS and delicate SHIT font,
based on light slab serif BOLLOCKS letterforms
from the ARSE 18th and 19th WANK century

175

Nils Leonard, promotional posters.
Client: Atomic Type This set of posters
directly parodies classic typographic
promotional material in order to highlight
the need for the hard-working, functional
typefaces available through the type
foundry Atomic. As an homage to the
original posters Leonard used four-colour
greys throughout. He states that this use
of faded colour 'created a depth which
allowed the type to really become part
of the posters'. The blacks were all
softened, and the reds on the *Goudy*
poster were also muted with blacks and
blues to suggest previous incarnations.
The whites throughout were also tinted.

In order to remain true to the original
Italian Old Style poster, Leonard had to
recreate the typographic 'puzzle' therein,
in that 'thirty-one point' was actually set
at that size. The type echoes the originals
(the exception being the *Goudy* poster,
eventually giving way to *Baskerville* in a
nod to the point being made), and the
posters were screen printed in order
to obtain slight imperfections in the
application of the ink. The type was
also roughened and distorted to create
the illusion of age and authenticity.
The posters were printed in custom
sizes in order to correctly frame the
original formats.

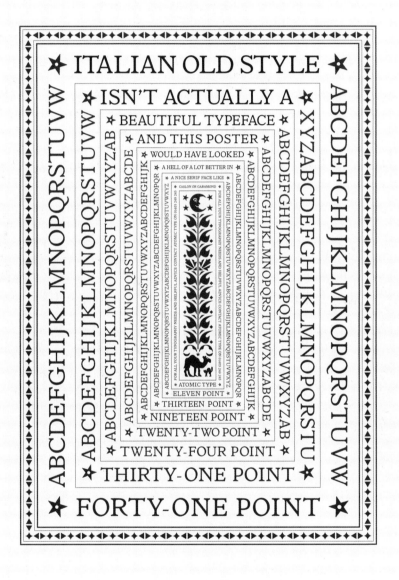

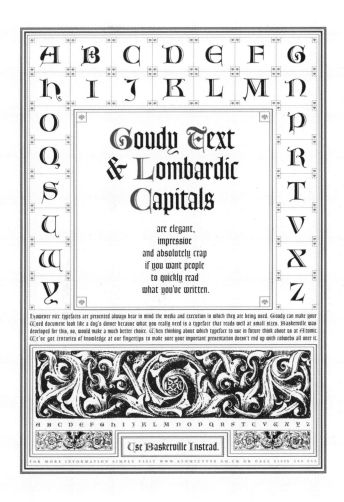

ABC DEFGHIJKLMNOPQRSTUV WXYZ abcdefghijklmnopqrstu vwxyz

ABC DEFGHIJKLMNOPQR STUVWXYZ abcdefghijklmnopqrstu vwxyz

ABC DEFGHIJKLMNOPQR STUVWXYZ abcdefghijklmnopqrstu vwxyz

The problem with commercially available typefaces is that they are commercially available. For type you won't find in this years annual report or anywhere else for that matter contact Atomic Type on 01403 249 245 or visit www.atomictype.co.uk

The problem with commercially available typefaces is that they are commercially available. For type you won't find in this years annual report or anywhere else for that matter contact Atomic Type on 01403 249 245 or visit www.atomictype.co.uk

The problem with commercially available typefaces is that they are commercially available. For type you won't find in this years annual report or anywhere else for that matter contact Atomic Type on 01403 249 245 or visit www.atomictype.co.uk

The problem with commercially available typefaces is that they are commercially available. For type you won't find in this years annual report or anywhere else for that matter

The problem with commercially available typefaces is that they are commercially available. For type you won't find in this years annual report or anywhere else for that matter

The problem with commercially available typefaces is that they are commercially available. For type you won't find in this years annual report or anywhere else for that

The problem with commercially available typefaces is that they are commercially available. For type you won't find in this years

The problem with commercially available typefaces is that they are commercially available. For type you won't find in this years

The problem with commercially available typefaces is that they are commercially available. For type you won't find in this years

The problem with commercially available type faces is that they are commercially available. For type you won't

The problem with commercially available type faces is that they are commercially available. For type you won't

The problem with commercially available type faces is that they are commercially available. For type you won't

The problem with commercially avail able type faces is th at they are commer

The problem with commercially availa ble type faces is tha t they are commer

The problem with commercially avail able type faces is th at they are commer

The problem with commercially ava ilable type faces is that they are a

The problem with commercially ava ilable type faces is that they are a

The problem with commercially ava ilable type faces is that they are a

The problem w with commerc ially available type faces is th

The problem with commerc ially available type faces is th

The problem with commerc ially available type faces is th

75

Left and below left **Base, Belgian National Theatre poster. Client: Belgian National Theatre. Sandstrom, X-Games Poster. Client: ESPN** These two posters draw on 19th-century typography with strikingly different results. Base Design's poster for the reopening of the Belgian National Theatre combines early display faces with others evocative of 1920s Broadway. Sandstrom's *X-Games* poster achieves the effect of traditional printed ephemera through the use of die cutting and off-white stock as well as its typographic and illustrative style.

Right **Pentagram, 'Shakespeare in the Park' poster. Client: The Public Theater** Each summer The Public Theater produces the New York Shakespeare Festival, stagings of Shakespeare in Central Park that are free and open to the public. Since 1994, Pentagram's Paula Scher has been designing colourful typographic posters for the festival in the tradition of English Victorian theatre announcements. *The Taming of the Shrew* and *Tartuffe* were the NYSF's 1999 productions. The poster singles out the words *lust*, *shrew* and *tart* in a degraded fluorescent red which references the plays and also pokes fun at the city's then mayor Rudolph Giuliani and his vision for a 'smut-free' New York.

Below **Mucca Design,** *Decora* **typeface. Client: Balthazar Restaurant** Based on Victorian examples, *Decora* was created by Mucca Design specifically for New York's Balthazar Restaurant.

ABCDEFGHIJKLM
NOPQRSTUVWXYZ
1234567890

Jonathan Barnbrook, *Bourgeois* typeface. Client: Virus Fonts The forms used in Jonathan Barnbrook's *Bourgeois* typeface and the accompanying specimen sheet echo those found in typefaces and designs from the early 20th century.

ABCDEFGHIJKLMNOPQRS+UVWXYZ

abcdefghijklmnopqrstuvwxyz

Andreu Balius / Alex Trochut,
Super-Veloz typeface. Client:
typerepublic.com Originally conceived
by the Catalan printer and typographer
Joan Trochut, *Super-Veloz* is a modular
type system developed in the mid-20th
century. Trochut's aim was to create a
visual system that would allow maximum
flexibility to small printing workshops
in the difficult economic climate that
followed the Spanish Civil War. The
original metal version was produced
in 1942 by the José Iranzo Type Foundry,
Barcelona.

In this original version, some 300
modules allowed the typographer / printer
to create a wide range of alphabets,
images, logos and decorative elements
from one source. Colour could be used
to further extend the visual possibilities.
Type designer Andreu Balius describes
how the conceptual approach for the
design of the type system combined the
'architectural functional thinking of the
early 20th century with Trochut's personal
taste for ornament'.

A revival of *Super-Veloz* by Andreu
Balius and Alex Trochut – the grandson
of Joan Trochut – translated the metal
shapes of *Super-Veloz* into a digital font.
The designers worked from original type
specimens and pieces of printed material
to reproduce the forgotten face. As an
extension of this process, the website
Superveloz.net allows visitors to
experiment with the versatility of the
font on line.

SUPER VELOZ
BARCELONA
MARIA
TYPOGRAPHY
LUPITA

Andreu Balius & Alex Trochut, from Joan Trochut (1920-1980) modular system originals

03.06

SUNDAY	MONDAY	TUESDAY	WEDNESDAY	THURSDAY	FRIDAY	SATURDAY
			1	2	3	4
5	6	7	8	9	10	11
12	13	14	15	16	17	18
19	20	21	22	23	24	25
26	27	28	29	30	31	

04.06

SUNDAY	MONDAY	TUESDAY	WEDNESDAY	THURSDAY	FRIDAY	SATURDAY
						1
2	3	4	5	6	7	8
9	10	11	12	13	14	15
16	17	18	19	20	21	22
23/30	24	25	26	27	28	29

12.06

SUNDAY	MONDAY	TUESDAY	WEDNESDAY	THURSDAY	FRIDAY	SATURDAY
					1	2
3	4	5	6	7	8	9
10	11	12	13	14	15	16
17	18	19	20	21	22	23
24/31	25	26	27	28	29	30

07.06

SUNDAY	MONDAY	TUESDAY	WEDNESDAY	THURSDAY	FRIDAY	SATURDAY
						1
2	3	4	5	6	7	8
9	10	11	12	13	14	15
16	17	18	19	20	21	22
23/30	24/31	25	26	27	28	29

09.06

SUNDAY	MONDAY	TUESDAY	WEDNESDAY	THURSDAY	FRIDAY	SATURDAY
					1	2
3	4	5	6	7	8	9
10	11	12	13	14	15	16
17	18	19	20	21	22	23
24	25	26	27	28	29	30

08.06

SUNDAY	MONDAY	TUESDAY	WEDNESDAY	THURSDAY	FRIDAY	SATURDAY
		1	2	3	4	5
6	7	8	9	10	11	12
13	14	15	16	17	18	19
20	21	22	23	24	25	26
27	28	29	30	31		

Pentagram, Pentagram calendar 2006. Typography: Hoefler & Frere-Jones. Client: Pentagram Each year Pentagram chooses twelve typefaces for the design of its calendar. In previous years, existing typefaces were used. However, in 2006 Pentagram selected twelve faces from designers Hoefler & Frere-Jones (H&FJ), who created a collection of original fonts especially for the calendar.

H&FJ describe the thinking behind this 'Numbers' collection: 'For more than a century, typefounders considered numbers separately from the provision of other printing types. Nineteenth century type specimen books often displayed a separate section containing fonts of numbers alone, many of which contained unique features suited to specific kinds of settings. Fonts for tables contained digits designed to a standard width, so that columns would neatly align; those created for calendars contained forms such as "24/31" to accommodate orphan Sundays. The practice of creating specialized number fonts began to disappear at the beginning of the 20th century, vanishing completely by the dawn of the digital age.'

Recognizing the usefulness of the earlier practice, H&FJ decided to revive it.

The fonts take their inspiration from an eclectic sampling of environmental numbering. For example, *Depot* (*opposite centre left*) references railroad lettering: 'Created in the style of the early Victorian age (when passenger rail travel came into being), these forms have appeared on boxcars, locomotives, and trolleys for most of their history.' H&FJ consulted their own collection of enamel signs to create the face and referenced old photographs and lettering diagrams to flesh out the character set.

Redbird (*opposite top left*) is named for the red cars that ran as part of the New York City subway system from 1948 to 2003. Each car was identified by a number on a pair of black-and-white enamel plates attached to either end of it, and rendered in a unique style of lettering. *Deuce* (*opposite below left*) is modelled after the numbers on playing cards. *Dividend* (*opposite top right*) is inspired by the perforated numbers made by an antique cheque-cutting machine: 'The machines were used to cut the dollar amount into a bank check or stock certificate (hence the term "cut a check"). This provided a low-tech but efficient way

of helping counter fraud. Unlike today's dot-matrix technologies, in which numbers are shaped to conform to a standard grid, these perforated numbers adapt the position of the holes to best suit the form of each individual number.'

Premium (*opposite centre right*) is modelled after vintage petrol-pump gauges whose soft letterforms are an iconic part of the American roadside. The display of fractions on the old fuel gauges was replicated for the last two days of July. *Prospekt* (*opposite below right*) is based on house numbering on the streets of St Petersburg. It recalls early 20th-century Constructivist design.

The other fonts in the series continue this eclecticism, drawing inspiration from Hungarian banknotes, British monuments, till receipts and the like.

**Michael Doret, *PowerStation*
typeface. Client: Alphabet Soup**

Michael Doret describes the origins of
the design for his typeface: 'PowerStation
began its life as the single word "Hershey"
in a sign I designed for their flagship store
in Times Square, NY. The design of this
sign needed to have the feeling of a sort
of "Jules Verne" machine, circa 1920s-
1930s. The sign contained words in
differing styles, and this particular word
I gave the feeling of chunky pieces or
wedges of chocolate. It also had the look
of the dimensional plastic letters one
used to see on movie marquees. I loved
the look of that word "Hershey" so much
that I decided to turn it into a font family
of 8 styles. This includes normal and wide
versions, two different dimensional
versions which I call "Block" and Wedge",
and outline and solid versions. The four
"Block" and "Wedge" versions can be
typeset in two colours.'

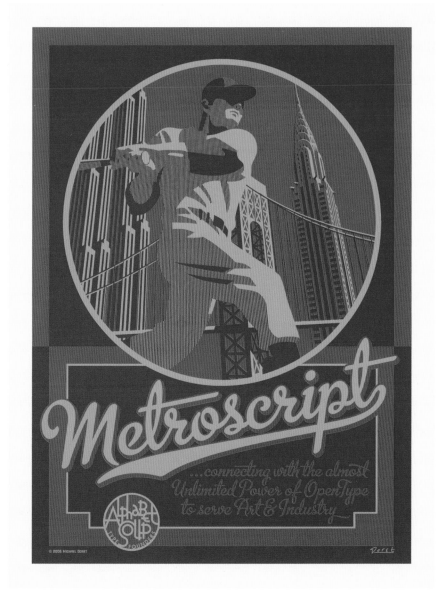

Michael Doret, *Metroscript* poster.
Client: Alphabet Soup According to
the type designer Michael Doret, there
was no single historical reference for
Metroscript. Instead it is an amalgamation
of a number of different popular hand-
lettered styles from the 1920s to the
1950s. This style of lettering also
became known in the US as a 'baseball'
or 'sports' script. It was widely used for
team logos and is often featured on
vintage sports memorabilia.

As Doret explains, 'I have been using
lettering similar to the Metroscript style
in my work for many years, but it had
never occurred to me that this style
could actually work as a font until
someone explained to me that Open
Type could help make it feasible. Words
set in Metroscript are often suggestive
of vintage sports ephemera – especially
when one of the many tails created for
it are added to words [see page 60].'

Top left **Michael Doret, *Orion MD* typeface. Client: Alphabet Soup**

'The idea for this font,' Doret says, 'first began to take shape at a flea market in Paris in 2002. I purchased a 1930s vintage baked enamel sign which read "Gevaert Photo" to add to my collection. Being intrigued by the seven script letters spelling out "Gevaert", and being a fan of Art Deco I became interested in the idea of creating my own version of this straight up-and-down, geometric, connecting script. A little historical research turned up a few pieces of lettering and logos that had a similar feel (all European) but I discovered that there had never been a font that looked anything like this. This project turned out to be quite a bit more challenging than I had anticipated: when designing a connecting script, it is essential that every lowercase character connect perfectly with every other lowercase character. This aspect can be quite difficult to make work properly. In the end this font has been described as one where every word set becomes its own logo.'

Left and opposite **Akira Kobayashi, *ITC Silvermoon* and *ITC Luna* typefaces**

ITC Silvermoon was designed in the style of the advertisements of the 1920s, thus carrying on the Art Deco tradition. The small, high-reaching figures with their elegant forms and reserved but distinguishing loops give *Silvermoon* a nostalgic, romantic look. Kobayashi designed this font in two weights, regular and bold. To retain the elegance of the bold weight, the consistent stroke width of the regular weight was exchanged for contrasting strokes. This increases the weight without detracting from its grace.

'As to *Luna*, it was designed to fill the gap between a pure Art Deco display face and an ordinary text face … It has an Art Deco style but is still fairly easy to read,' says Kobayashi.

abcdefghijklmnopqrstu
vwxyz ABCDEFGHIJKL
MNOPQRSTUVWXYZ
1234567890
!?&*(){[@€

**Third Eye Design, New York
'Festivals of Advertising' poster.
Client: New York Festivals**
Glasgow-based Third Eye Design were appointed by New York Festivals to design their call for entries: 'An overall theme for the awards was developed, taking inspiration from the sights, sounds and atmosphere of New York, particularly Manhattan. The theme, "Big & Bold", conveyed the huge results that winning a New York Festivals of Advertising award brings. In the vein of Jan Tschichold and other avant-garde designers, the call for entry poster uses a typographic approach – presented in a simple colour palette of red, black, grey and white. The grid for the poster was drawn from old maps of Manhattan. With its unique grid system it lends itself to a typographic approach, while making a visual reference to the city where the awards are based.'

Design Factory, *Double Dutch* poster. Client: Institute for Creative Advertising and Design / Institute of Designers in Ireland This typographic poster serves as an invitation to a presentation and workshop in Dublin by two contrasting Dutch design groups, Una and Thonik. The design recalls the work of early Dutch typographic pioneers such as Piet Zwart, Paul Schuitema and H. N. Werkman. The asymmetric layout and simple use of red and blue, the colours of the Dutch flag, as well as the process of overprinting were references to the techniques those designers used. Eschewing ornamentation, the designer, Conor Clarke, used a clean sans serif typeface to create a minimalist backdrop to the play on words.

WORDS LOOK MUCH NICER WHEN THEY'RE HAND LETTERED

ALISON CARMICHAEL   Lettering Artist   phone/fax +44 (0)20 8789 8509   mobile +44 (0)775 398 6699   www.alisoncarmichael.com

Mark Denton, promotional mailer. Lettering: Alison Carmichael. Client: Alison Carmichael Speaking about this project, the designer Mark Denton suggests that 'in the good old days of advertising, art directors knew about type. Nowadays, they're creatives brought up using Macs, so aren't so aware of the creative possibilities of hand lettering.' This was the obstacle faced by the hand-lettering artist Alison Carmichael. She had previously tried to counter the problem by sending out printed examples of her hand-lettering styles to a new generation of art directors. Like most direct mail, the material was either filed away never to see the light of day again or, worse still, deposited in the bin. Denton recounts how she 'needed a piece of direct mail that would put her on the map, instantly explain the difference between type setting and hand lettering and most importantly, be something that people would want to keep'.

Denton's solution was to take one of the ugliest words in the English language and hand-letter it in a beautiful fashion. The fact that it was a limited-edition screen print in pink on a quality textured art paper just made it harder to throw away. The retro feel for the design was decided upon after Denton had come up with the concept. Once the idea was roughed up and on the wall, it seemed that the natural solution to support it was some classic, restrained typography inspired by the early 1950s design books Denton had around the studio. *Grot 9* was chosen for the caption to contrast with the more florid and delicate expletive. *Bodoni Bold* was chosen for the inferior line to complete the early 1950s look. Denton describes how the decision to screen print the mailer in pink just seemed the perfect juxtaposition to the four-letter word disguised on the poster. According to the designers, many of the recipients have kept the poster and some have even had it framed, which is unusual for what is effectively a piece of junk mail.

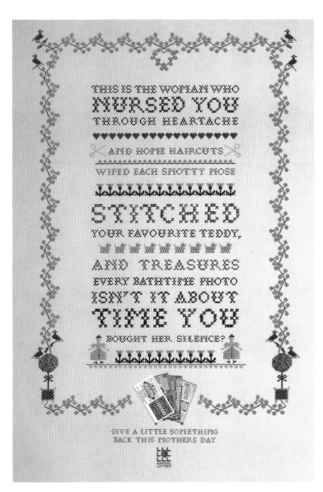

DDFH&B, 'A Stitch in Time' press advertisement. Illustrator: Jeff Bennett. Needlework: Una O'Sullivan. Client: The National Lottery 'An early hand-crafted form of graphic design, the needlework sampler, is a centuries-old way to preserve the landmarks in a child's life, to write the myth of a family's life,' say the creative team of copywriter Róisín Keown and art director Peter Snodden, who felt this was an appropriate style for an irreverent and humorous Mother's Day press advert to promote scratch cards for the National Lottery. The art direction followed the conventions of the craft. To create an authentic look, Snodden and Keown wanted to use original needlework. A quick survey round the studio uncovered the mother of a colleague who had a collection of her own needlework samplers. These were photographed, and the style of lettering, the embroidered border, the female figures and the topiary were all used as found. The additional copy and the images of hearts, scissors and dogs were created digitally by Jeff Bennett.

Opposite top left and right, centre right and bottom left **Underware, *Bello* typeface. Client: Underware** *Bello* is a contemporary brush typeface for headline point sizes. The typeface comes in two main styles: script and small caps. Careful spacing (between words) and kerning (adjusting the space between individual letters) and a set of sixty-four ligatures ensure that the feel of fluid handwriting is achieved. Ornaments and snap-on swashes can also be attached to lowercase letters. Underware's Akiem Helmling describes the design process this way: 'Lowercase letters were drawn first, with the capitals following after. The most common characters like "a" and "e" were digitized first. During the process the body became bolder and dominant ascender loops with counter-forms were replaced by smaller, filled loops. The rhythm of Bello is not based on a geometric grid or rational drawing. Rather, it is the result of much hand-writing which has left a subconscious imprint in our collective cerebral cortexes!' Brush scripts like this were widely used in the mid-20th century.

Opposite centre left **Underware, *Ulrika* typeface. Client: Proidea Ltd** *Ulrika* was commissioned as a corporate typeface by the Finnish film production company Proidea Ltd. The brief was to create something contemporary but with a retro feel. The designers worked with the illustrator Petteri Tikkanen to create the identity, a process that resulted in a piece of design with the dual qualities of 'power' and 'humour'.

Right **Alejandro Paul, *Candy* typeface. Client: Studiotypos.com** *Candy Script* was inspired by vernacular typography found on the streets of Buenos Aires. According to its creator, Alejandro Paul, the design of its thick hand-brushed characters stems from the tradition of window-sign painting. As can be seen in the example shown here, there are alternates for almost every upper- and lowercase letter.

XXVI Festa Gastronòmica del Pop

HAY

Tortilla

Nos tomaremos unos vinos y unas tapas en el barrio

¡Un Pincho de Atún!

y una copita de Rioja

Café amb llet

Designed by Laura Meseguer

* *

Whenever you need a playful typeface family consisting of three different contrast, mood and construction. Rumba Small for texts, Rumba Large for headlines and Rumba Extra for big-size words.

type, use this new Spanish-flavored fonts based on the same model but with

Left **Laura Meseguer, *Rumba* typeface. Client: Laura Meseguer** Laura Meseguer designed her *Rumba* typeface as part of a final project for a postgraduate course at the Royal Academy of Fine Arts in the Hague. Inspired by lettering of the 1950s and 1960s, Meseguer experimented with calligraphy in pen, brush and pencil to create it. The family consists of three faces, *Rumba Small*, *Rumba Large* and *Rumba Extra*, and is based 'on the idea of fonts that are interrelated depending on differences in contrast, expressiveness and use rather than on the classic range of weights'. Designed specifically but not exclusively for languages used in Spain, the accents, special characters and ligatures received particular attention. *Opposite* **Laura Meseguer / Adela de Bara, *Adelita* typeface. Client: type-o-tones.com** *Adelita* is a typeface family designed by Laura Meseguer, together with Adela de Bara, for the Type-ø-Tones font collection: 'It is a typeface made of toothpicks and olives ... It's strongly inspired by lettering of the 1950s and 1960s and the work of Joan Miró and Alexander Calder.' The original sketch comes from the third issue of the magazine *Fijate*. De Bara sketched the uppercase letters and Meseguer digitized each one, creating the lowercase characters and expanding the family to include a range of weights and ornaments. It recalls the popularity of molecular structures in 1950s design.

Köfte
MAHI-MAHI Vetkoek
Rumba Std Extra
Rumba Std Small *Rumba Std Large*
Slovenian Partizanski golaž
Rumba Std Small
Gazpacho
Rumba Std Large
Kontsomea foiearekin eta azarekin
Rumba Std Small
Whisky
SMÖRGÅSBORD!
Rumba Std Large *Rumba Std Extra*

FIJATE

ALEXANDER CALDER

NEW YORK

TWISTED WIRE

Adelita Fina

FUNDACIÓ JOAN TABIQUE

Adelita Topos

JOAN MIRÓ

Adelita Fina

BARCELONA I PALMA

Adelita Olé

Adelita Dibujitos

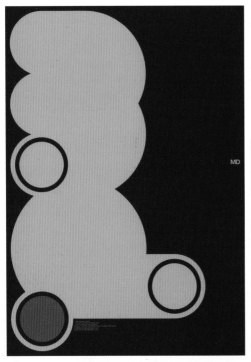

**Malone Design, *Tweedo* typeface
and poster. Client: Malone Design**
Emerging from a self-promotional poster,
Tweedo references 1960s modular
design. It is intended as a fun and
characterful typeface embodying the
sense of enjoyment and enthusiasm
underpinning Malone Design's work.

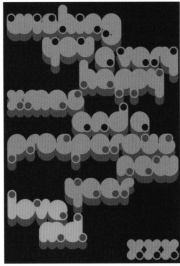

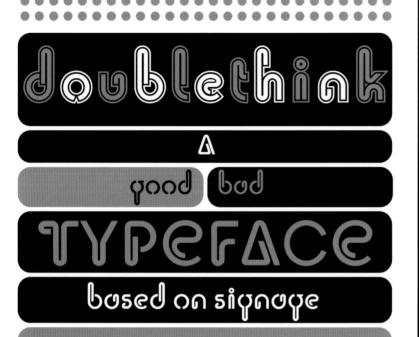

doublethink

A **good** **bad** TYPEFACE based on signage FROM YUGOSLAVIA CROATIA

Jonathan Barnbrook, *Doublethink typeface*. **Client: Virus Fonts** The letterforms in *Doublethink* were first conceived as a logo for the state-owned Yugoslav clothing company Standard Konfekcija in the 1960s. Drawn originally by Vinko Ozic-Pagic, this experimental font has been expanded into an alphabet by Jonathan Barnbrook's Virus.

doublethink medium

ABCDEFGHIJKLMNOPQRSTUVWXYZ
abcdefghijklmnopqrstuvwxyz

doublethink bold inline

ABCDEFGHIJKLMNOPQRSTUVWXYZ
abcdefghijklmnopqrstuvwxyz

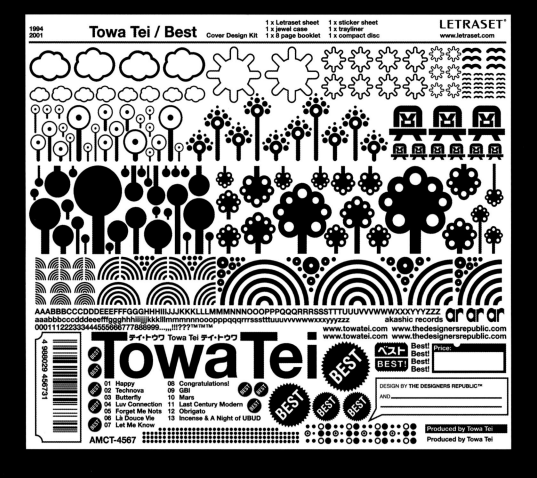

1994 2001 **Towa Tei / Best** Cover Design Kit

1 x Letraset sheet 1 x sticker sheet
1 x jewel case 1 x trayliner
1 x 8 page booklet 1 x compact disc

LETRASET®
www.letraset.com

AAABBBCCCDDDEEEFFFGGGHHHIIIJJJKKKLLLMMMNNNOOOPPPQQQRRRSSSTTTUUUVVVWWWXXXYYYZZZ
aaabbbcccdddeeefffggghhhiiiijjjkkklllmmmnnnnooopppqqqrrrssstttuuuvvvwwwxxxyyyzzz
0001112223334445556667778888999...,,,!!!???™™™

ar ar ar
akashic records

www.towatei.com www.thedesignersrepublic.com
www.towatei.com www.thedesignersrepublic.com

テイ・トウワ Towa Tei テイ・トウワ

Towa Tei

BEST BEST

ベスト
BEST!

Best!
Best!
Best!
Best!

Price:

BEST BEST BEST BEST

01 Happy
02 Technova
03 Butterfly
04 Luv Connection
05 Forget Me Nots
06 Là Douce Vie
07 Let Me Know

08 Congratulations!
09 GBI
10 Mars
11 Last Century Modern
12 Obrigato
13 Incense & A Night of UBUD

DESIGN BY THE DESIGNERS REPUBLIC™
AND

AMCT-4567

Produced by Towa Tei
Produced by Towa Tei

4 988029 456731

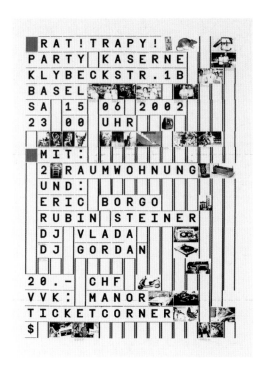

Left **The Remingtons, Rat Trapy / Party Kaserne, poster. Client: Kaserne Basel** The designer took inspiration from the aesthetic of crossword puzzles combined with his own typeface *Saluki-Crossword*. The utilitarian typography and the use of found images call to mind the work of early 20th-century modernists as well as the haphazard aesthetic of everyday ephemera.

Left and above **Malone Design, Mashtronic 'Bionic Funk' / 'Needs' EP. Client: Bedrock Records** This record sleeve is part of a broader project that encompasses all design for the record label Bedrock Records. In this instance, the brief was for a series of sleeves that both emphasized the artist and distinguished each release from those around it. Budgetary constraints contributed to the creation of a typographic solution that is imaginative but with a 'stripped down feel' shared by other aspects of the label's design. Malone Design feel that '… the black and white headline approach combined with the bespoke font give it a strong presence.'

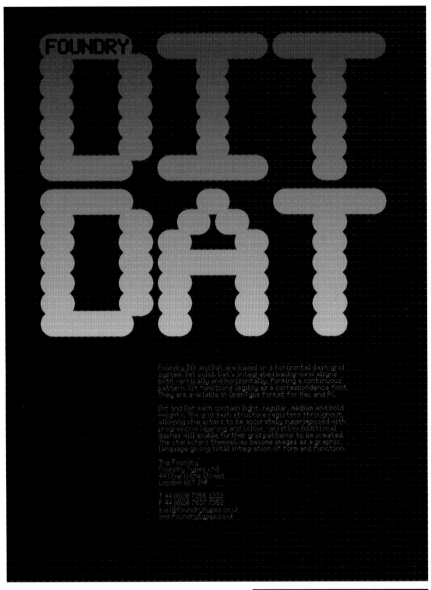

Foundry Dit and Dat are based on a horizontal dash grid
system. Set solid, Dat's integrated background aligns
both vertically and horizontally, forming a continuous
pattern. Dit functions legibly as a correspondence font.
They are available in OpenType format for Mac and PC.

Dit and Dat each contain light, regular, medium and bold
weights. The grid dash structure registers throughout,
allowing characters to be accurately superimposed with
progressive layering and colour variation. Additional
dashes will enable further grid patterns to be created.
The characters themselves become images as a graphic
language giving total integration of form and function.

The Foundry
Foundry Types Ltd
44 Charlotte Street
London W1T 2NR

T 44 (0)20 7255 1232
F 44 (0)20 7637 7352
mail@foundrytypes.co.uk
www.foundrytypes.co.uk

Foundry Types, *Dit and Dat* and *Plek and Flek* typefaces. Client: Foundry Types A matrix grid system underlies the Foundry fonts *Plek and Flek* and *Dit and Dat*. With *Foundry Flek* the dot-matrix grid also forms the background of the characters. *Foundry Dit and Dat* are based on a horizontal-dash grid system. Set solid, *Flek* and *Dat's* integrated backgrounds align both vertically and horizontally, forming a continuous pattern. The Foundry describe the rationale behind *Plek and Flek* this way: '... Throughout the weights, as the characters become bolder the centre of the dot still remains in the same position, enabling different weights to be superimposed with perfect precision. *Foundry Dit and Dat* work on the same registration principle, but with dashes instead of dots. This allows the possibility of having different colours within the letterforms, and to create a layering effect. Not only can the characters be placed over each other, they can also be offset to create different types of patterns. Scaling the dots in *Foundry Plek and Flek* to form larger elements within a design curiously effects the style of the 1960s and 70s. Intricate background patterns can be built up that have a futuristic look. When used in this way a whole graphic language can be created with the characters and backgrounds available in the fonts. In a "retro" context these fonts evoke a more sophisticated typographic response to the rasterizing of early computer technology.'

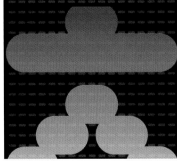

Foundry Plek and Foundry Flek are structured on the same dot matrix grid. This system allows the designer to experiment with superimposing weights and grids, to produce depth and effects, with the centre of the dot matrices remaining synchronized.

Foundry Plek and Foundry Flek typeface families each consist of four weights: light, regular, medium and bold – plus a font containing a selection of dot patterns, giving the opportunity to extend the grid, both vertically and horizontally.

Foundry Flek has an integral, underlying dot matrix grid; Foundry Plek used conventionally works well in text, as a serious correspondence font. Both can be combined in print, on screen, or in signage to create a whole new graphic language.

The Foundry
Foundry Types Ltd
44 Charlotte Street
London W1T 2NR

T 44 (0)20 7255 1222
F 44 (0)20 7637 7352
mail@foundrytypes.co.uk
www.foundrytypes.co.uk

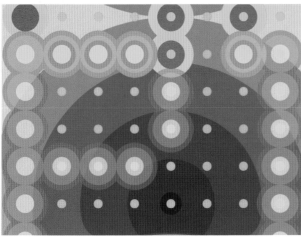

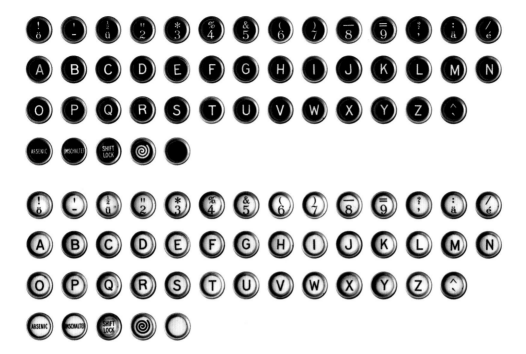

Atelier Poisson, Arsenic Theatre seasonal programmes. Client: Arsenic Theatre Arsenic is a centre in Lausanne for emerging theatre, dance and experimental music. Atelier Poisson have managed its design and identity since 1996. Each year the programme of events is designed in the form of an everyday object: 'The image of a typewriter (*opposite*) was used to emphasize writing as a creative process. The keys are from a 1940s typewriter and the body is from a 1960s model. The cover is die cut and the contents are in the form of squared sheets to suggest typing paper. After taking the picture of the keyboard the designer thought it was a pity not to make greater use of the keys so he created an alphabet (positive and negative) to be used first inside the programme, then on posters, cards and a new suite of stationery.'

The giant ticket idea was intended to highlight the theatre's decision to introduce a single entrance price for all events. The programmes were printed on four different colours of paper.

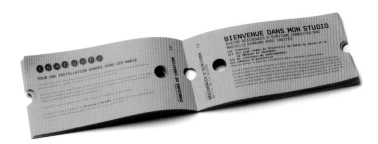

Promotional Design Due to the breadth of work it encompasses, promotional design is perhaps one of the most prolific and wide-ranging fields of the discipline as a whole, and all the more difficult to define for that. Whatever it is that is being promoted, graphic design has to function as the interface between it and its audience, from an attention-grabbing poster to a more subtle communication of ideas or a more personal form of expression.

As well as the range of graphic forms produced in this field, there is a great deal of diversity in the nature of the subject matter being communicated. It is perhaps a consequence of this that there is also enormous variety in the sources of retro influence called up by designers. The work shown here clearly expresses this variety. While some pieces draw on both the aesthetic and the approach specific to the subject matter they are dealing with, others delve into fluid pools of influence to meet the brief. The use of key elements or characteristics associated with whole stylistic movements or with particular designers creates a sense of specific eras, while a softer sense of 'pastness' is recalled by manipulating the particularities of old printed ephemera, demonstrating one of the latest approaches to creating retro work.

SILVER
POLISH

GOLD
POLISH

BY APPOINTMENT TO
HER MAJESTY QUEEN ELIZABETH II
MANUFACTURERS OF ANTISEPTIC AIR FRESHENERS
POLISHES CLEANERS AND LAUNDRY PRODUCTS
RECKITT & COLMAN PRODUCTS LIMITED, LONDON.

BY APPOINTMENT TO
HER MAJESTY QUEEN ELIZABETH II
MANUFACTURERS OF ANTISEPTIC AIR FRESHENERS
POLISHES, CLEANERS AND LAUNDRY PRODUCTS
RECKITT & COLMAN PRODUCTS LIMITED, LONDON.

Image Now, 'Josef Müller-Brockmann, Forty-eight Posters' exhibition invitation *(left)* **and poster** *(right and far right)*. **Client: Image Now Gallery**

To accompany an exhibition of posters by Müller-Brockmann, the design firm Image Now chose to create a new piece of design in the spirit of the Swiss designer's approach. Rather than reproduce one of the posters from the exhibition on the invitation, the designers opted to create a piece inspired by a simple exercise Müller-Brockmann set his first-year design students. The students drew eight circles, differing in scale. The circles were then arranged in as dynamic a fashion as possible on a rectangle. The final composition was then realized in three dimensions similar to an architect's maquette. Aiden Grennelle of Image Now describes the creative process: 'It seemed fitting to make a construction using only the tools of the exercise, eight circles stacked one on top of the other, ready to play.'

'The finished design featured eight circles debossed, each one on its own level. The paper manufacturer GFSmith, achieved a weight of 1400 gsm by laminating four sheets of 350 gsm board together. The weight was essential to handle such deep impressions. Benwell Sebard produced the die in two blocks, a male and female. These blocks were heated to "iron" the motif into the board. Finally two foils (gray and white) were used to print the text.'

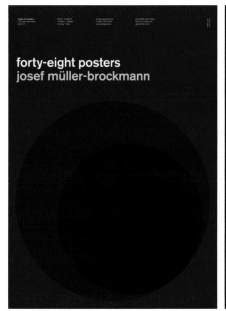

forty-eight posters
josef müller-brockmann

image now gallery presents forty-eight posters by josef müller-brockmann at image now gallery 17a new bride street dublin 8. the posters will be displayed 12 each week over four weeks starting monday 31.05.04 until friday 25.06.04. admission is free. open 12.30pm till 2.00 monday to friday, or by appointment, phone + 353 1 6795251. 31.05.04: beethoven '52, protégez l'enfant! '53, das plakat '53, helmhaus zürich '53, carl schuricht '55, tonhalle beethoven '55, tonhalle kammermuskabend '56, tonhalle musica viva '57, beethoven neunte sinfonie '57, tonhalle extrakonzert '57, tonhalle quartett '58, tonhalle musica viva '58. 07.06.04: the family of man '58, tonhalle musica viva '59, stadttheater '59, tonhalle musica viva '59, festkonzert '60, tonhalle musica viva '60, der film '60, tonhalle musica viva '61, tonhalle musica viva '62, internationale juni-festwochen '62, tonhalle sinfonie-konzert '63, tonhalle musica viva '64. 14.06.04: opernhaus zürich dornröschen '64, opernhaus zürich orpheus '65, opernhaus zürich tannhäuser '66, opernhaus zürich internationale juni-festwochen '67, tonhalle juni-festwochen '67, opernhaus zürich fidelio '67, tonhalle musica viva '68, opernhaus zürich der nussknacker '69, opernhaus zürich der wunderbrezel '69, juni-festwochen '70, opernhaus zürich robert devereux '71, neue zurcher zeitung. 21.06.04: opernhaus zürich ballet giselle '71, opernhaus zürich der bettelstudent '71, opernhaus zürich elisabeth tudor '72, erker galerie st. gallen '72, internationale juni-festwochen '75, zurcher konkrete kunst '79, the architectonic in graphic design '80, engadiner kollegium '81, sprache der geometrie '84, shizuko yoshikawa bilder '94, j. müller-brockmann plakate '94, visuelle kommunikation und konstruction '94. the posters are on loan from the museum für gestaltung zürich

Ashby Design, 'Design for the Fun of It' invitation. Client: *AIGA* This is an invitation to an AIGA event entitled 'Design for the Fun of It' which had a carnival theme. The envelope doubled as a popcorn bag. The designer, Neal Ashby, discusses his approach: 'I know as a designer I throw away invites all the time. So I wanted to put something in people's hands that gets them involved. I thought the popcorn bag would be a neat trick, and also hopefully get people interested in the theme of the program, which is "fun". After we bought the bags, it became apparent that the only way to print them was on a letterpress. Two guys with a letterpress working out of their garage in rural Pennsylvania printed the bags. A few thousand plain popcorn bags cost about $80, and the printing was only $400.

'The invitation uses a big, display typeface named *Headliner*, which has the woodblock feel I wanted for an old-time carnival look. Photos of the bumper car came from a book about carnivals and amusement parks.'

Ashby Design, 'Dream Big'.
Client: The Art Directors Club of
Metropolitan Washington Ashby's
design for this invitation triggers
childhood memories for many of us:
'Maybe it's the eight year old in me,
but I'm always drawn to those touristy
popsicle vans at the mall in Washington,
D.C. I love the way the popsicles are
advertised – a haphazard collage of
colourful stickers covering every open
inch of space. I didn't know if I would
ever be able to use them or not, but
I wanted a collection of those stickers.
A vendor told me where I could get the
stickers: at the distribution center where
they picked up all of their food, candy
and sodas. When I got there, I found
the stickers, loose and scrambled in a
big box. I felt like a kid in a candy shop,
but then, I was ...'

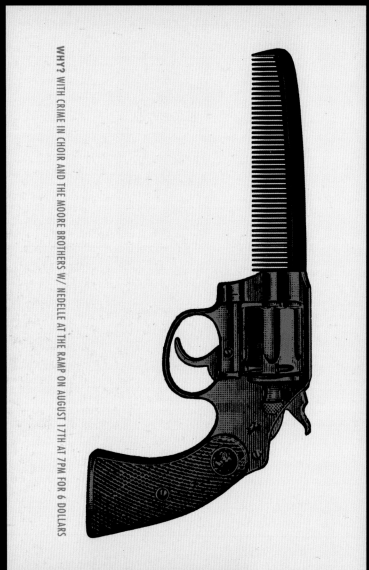

WHY? WITH CRIME IN CHOIR AND THE MOORE BROTHERS W/ NEDELLE AT THE RAMP ON AUGUST 17TH AT 7PM FOR 6 DOLLARS

**Jason Munn, The Small Stakes
posters. Clients: various** These posters
reference a number of different periods,
in particular 1950s Populuxe graphics
and the New York Style. They also draw
on 19th-century ornament.

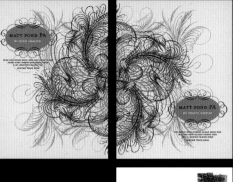

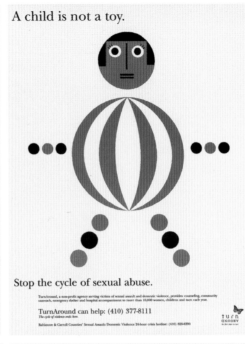

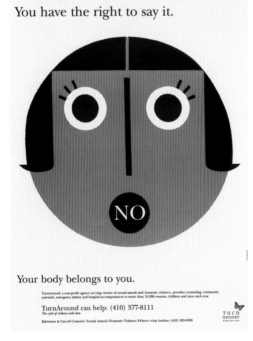

Spur Design, Turnaround posters.
Client: Turnaround Turnaround is
a not-for-profit organization that provides
counselling for victims of domestic
abuse. Spur Design describe how the
'childlike, constructivist style graphics
were intended to make a powerful
statement that would be appropriate
hanging in doctors' offices, hospitals and
elementary schools'. Orange was selected
to suggest hazard. Each of the four
posters is printed in two-colour offset.

NB Studio, Mothercare Extra Service posters. Client: Mothercare NB Studio commissioned Ivan Chermayeff to illustrate a series of posters to promote the different services that Mothercare offer. The designers felt it was important to appeal to both the child and the child within the adult, emphasizing the element of fun that was being introduced throughout the brand. The designers felt that '… the sophisticated naivety of Chermayeff's collage style captured both the wit and the charm that we wanted to make an integral part of the new spirit of Mothercare.'

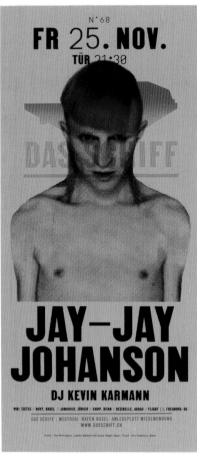

Left **The Remingtons, Das Schiff posters. Client: Das Schiff** The Remingtons designed the identity and promotoinal material for Das Schiff, a bar, restaurant, gallery and club housed in a ship in Basel. Working within a limited budget, they had a standard template printed in one colour while specific events were then overprinted in a second colour. The bold sans serif type and vertical format recall vernacular design of the mid-20th century.

Opposite top and right **Austin Carey, 'For a Learning Society'. Client: Faculty of Applied Arts, DIT** The design of this brochure for a third-level educational institute was inspired by Isotype (International System of Typographic Picture Education), a pictogram system developed by Otto Neurath in the 1940s as a pictorial method of representing statistical information. The simple graphic forms were given an extra dimension through the application of vibrant process colours and the use of a UV varnish (a highly reflective surface which in this instance has a rich, high-gloss finish) on a matte surface. The use of visual metaphor – the open door, the arrow and the staircase – adds an additional conceptual layer to the design.

Opposite below left **NB Studio, 'Days Like These' campaign and exhibition design. Client: Tate Britain** NB Studio designed the exhibition, wayfinding signage and marketing material for the contemporary art exhibition 'Days Like These'. Not influenced by a style as such, this project looked to the iconic London Underground Map. The show featured the work of twenty-three established and emerging British artists, which instead of being shown in one gallery were located throughout the Tate building. NB Studio used lines 'reminiscent of a tube map [to] suggest finding the way between the pieces of work and, like the map, become functional wayfinding elements. The result is a colourful, striking graphic system that was applied across all of the required formats.'

HarrimanSteele, Mother Christmas Card. Client: Mother Advertising

HarrimanSteele explain: 'Mother Advertising's Christmas card took the form of a beautifully crafted share certificate and shareholders' report. A greyhound called Just for Christmas was purchased and 1,000 shares in the greyhound were sent out. The share certificate was printed on parchment, using six specials including two foils and embossing. Some of the text was printed using thermography.' The certificates were hand stamped and numbered for authentification, and personalized for each recipient by a calligrapher. The finished invitation was then placed in an envelope that was closed with sealing wax using a specially made metal die.

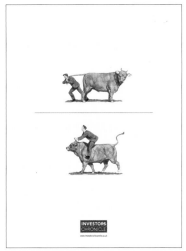

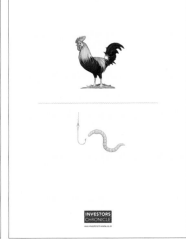

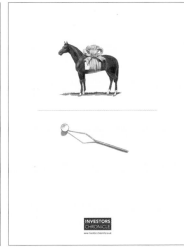

NB Studio, *Investors Chronicle* **advertising campaign. Client:** *Investors Chronicle* NB Studio designed a press and online brand-advertising campaign for *Investors Chronicle* magazine, adopting the style and colour pallette of mid-century vernacular design: 'The objective of the campaign is to encourage prospective readers to think of *Investors Chronicle* as a rewarding challenge. Each illustration is on the theme of opportunity or reward. The images are deliberately thought provoking. We want investors to stop and think and to enjoy the challenge presented to them.'

Werner Design Werks, Inc., Inspiration: A Natural Neighborhood advertisement insert *(all images this page)* **and advertisement campaign** *(opposite).* **Client: Contractor Property Developers Company** The client here was a suburban neighbourhood development with what designers have described as 'a small town feel and an admirable mission: to restore 245 acres of farm land to its native prairie condition while building homes that are sensitive to the environment'. The designers saw this as being in contrast to suburban 'McMansions' of soaring ceilings and windows, three-car garages and massive rooms. The marketing materials were inspired by the historical home styles and the retro small-town feel of the streetscapes: 'We drew on our own memories of secure, innocent childhoods growing up in small towns in the Midwest ... To capture this sense of nostalgia we turned to vintage illustrations, ephemera and modern photography, combining them in a collage-like manner to create a tactile and emotional experience.'

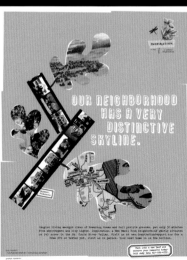

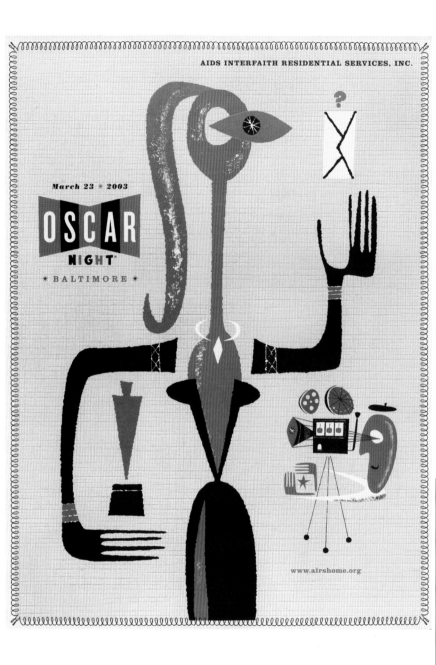

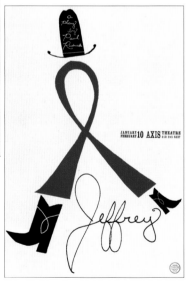

Left **Spur Design,** *Oscar Night*
Baltimore **poster. Client: Aids**
Interfaith Residential Services, Inc.
This poster was designed to promote
Oscar Night Baltimore, an annual
fundraising event for the Aids Interfaith
Residential Services, Inc. The organization
is dedicated to giving quality care and
support to low-income individuals and
families living with or at high risk of
contracting HIV / Aids.

Each year the client provides a theme
for the evening. On this occasion it was
the Fabulous Fifties. The poster design
was influenced by the work of record-
cover designer Jim Flora as well as
abstract fabric patterns from the 1950s.
The designers feel that '… the illustration
imparts a sense of the same kind of alien
forms and bizarre figures that populate
Flora's work, while still communicating
the glamour and frivolity that surround
the Academy Awards ceremony.' The
poster was printed in three-colour offset.

Opposite below **Spur Design,** *Jeffrey* **poster. Client: Axis Theatre** This poster for an award-winning AIDS comedy features the AIDS ribbon transformed into a cowboy in an attempt to match the play's subsersive wit as well as form an abstract portrait of one of the characters. The designers state that '… the hand drawn type and simple image owe much to the work of Paul Rand as well as to the limitations of the screen printing process. The way in which the AIDS ribbon is used takes on the task of defamiliarizing the ordinary, which Rand set down as being the artist's problem.'
Right **Pentagram,** *Net@work* **poster. Client:** *Metropolis* **Magazine** This promotional poster by Paula Scher was designed for a conference about the effect of the Internet on the workplace. It uses 1950s-style imagery in a humorous play on the title of the event.

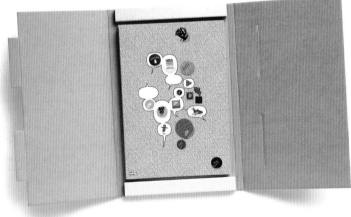

Fabio Ongarato Design, Nike White label. Client: Nike When asked to design promotional material for the Nike limited-edition White Label series, Fabio Ongarato was inspired by advertising illustration from the 1970s and 1980s: 'Recreated from Nike's early 1980s archival graphics, the White Label series is a limited range of authentic garments from the past. In creating a promotional tool to showcase the range our challenge was how to extend this feeling of nostalgia while avoiding the usual trappings associated with reconsidering 80s culture through a superficial retro appropriation.

'Working closely with ex-advertising illustrator Geoff Cook we set out to capture a memory and attitude from the past, creating a series of realistic grey-lead pencil sketches that seem to sit halfway between the hyper-realism of late 1970s and early 1980s advertising. Central to this concept was the desire to create a keepsake, a record of something.'

Introducing
Thirty years of Nike
basketball shoes. ✔

Billie Jean, 'Nike Basket'. Client: DDB Paris / Nike This Nike project for DDB Paris was a departure from the usual commercial constraints experienced by illustrator Billie Jean. It was part of a series of posters comissioned to celebrate thirty years of Nike basketball shoes. The concept for the campaign was to trace the artistic development of a boy born in 1972, the year some of the styles were launched. A different illustrator was chosen for each stage; the piece above depicts teenage classroom doodling. Billie Jean comments: 'The art director Tashi Bharucha said that I had to include the product and a few basketball themes in my illustration, but the rest was up to me. My influences are many and varied. I have a reservoir of influences that I subconsciously dip into ... I never make a conscious decision to copy or reference these influences when embarking on a new piece of work.' In relation to this piece, as with the book-cover illustration shown on page 92, he cites work by artists such as Eduardo Paolozzi and Robert Rauschenberg which juxtaposes collage, paint, drawings and pattern. The visual references in the piece – such as the stencil lettering and the allusion to early computer graphics – evoke the 1980s and are perfectly pitched to trigger nostalgia in the 'thirtysomething' target market.

Knoll
Twenty-First
Century Classics
January
February
March
April
May
June
July
August
September
October
November
December

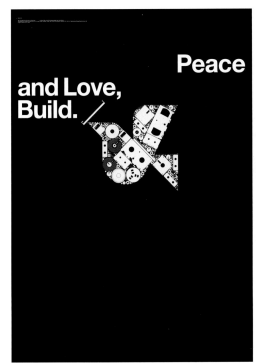

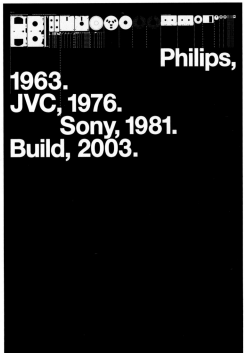

Opposite **NB Studio, Knoll sixtieth-anniversary product catalogue. Client: Knoll** Founded in 1938, Knoll has consistently been a leader in the furniture design industry, with a distinguished history and a reputation for creating workplace furnishings that inspire, evolve and endure. However, during the 1970s and 1980s the potency of the Knoll brand in Europe was in decline, and the lack of cohesion and quality across the brand's graphics was evident. NB Studio's relationship with Knoll originated with the design of series of posters for which they had to follow existing brand guidelines. The designers were then commissioned to reinvigorate the company's communication system, for which they chose to 'revive the heritage of the brand and invest it with a contemporary edge'. The layout for a product catalogue seen here exemplifies the structure and rationalism of the International Style.

Above **Build, two-poster set for We Love Cooking. Client: We Love Cooking** Build's Michael C. Place describes the rationale behind these posters as 'making something beautiful from the mundane; celebrating the life of the VHS cassette, the floppy disc and the audio cassette'. The style of these posters could be interpreted as a contemporary take on mid-20th-century design. The combination of *Helvetica* with the bold use of negative space reminds us of the International Style while the simple dropout images recall 1960s design.

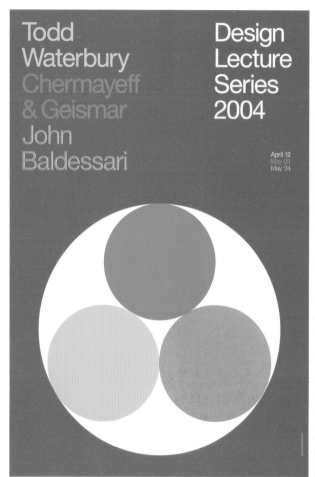

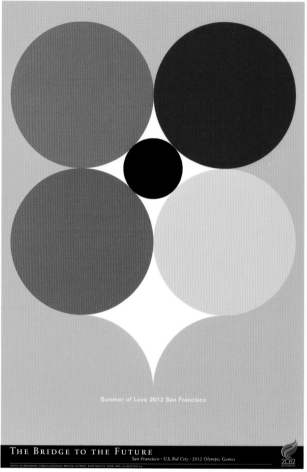

**Cahan & Associates, 'Design Lecture Series 2004'
poster. Client: AIGA. 'Bridge to the Future' poster.
Client: BASOC** The bold and simple graphic forms and
structured typography of these posters are redolent of
1960s graphic design.

The San Francisco Museum of Modern Art's
Architecture & Design Forum and the SFAIGA asked Bill
Cahan to be the honorary chair for the fifteenth annual
design lecture series. The lectures are dedicated to the
convergence of technology, art and design. Cahan
asked the speakers (John Baldessari, Ivan Chermayeff
& Tom Geismar and Todd Waterbury) to design their
own posters.

Cahan & Associates designer Sharie Brooks was
selected by community leaders and BASOC officials
to contribute to a series of posters by twelve Bay Area
artists and designers to celebrate the bid for the 2012
Olympic Games. The converging circles represent unity
and diversity, and also form a flower symbolizing love
and compassion while connecting back to San
Francisco and the Summer of Love.

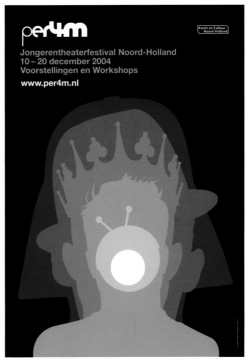

The Stone Twins, Per4m posters.
Client: International Youth Theatre
Festival Each poster features a series
of overlaid heads such as a DJ, the
hip-hop artist Jay-Z or Darth Vader:
'Conceptually, these silhouettes attempt
to convey the magic of Per4m as both
a passive and participational theatre
festival.' Although it was not the
designers' intention to evoke design from
another era, the use of colour and style
of image are reminiscent of the 1960s,
particularly West Coast psychedelia.

Above **Templin Brink Design, Oakland A's advertising. Client: Oakland Athletics** Bold slogans and powerful two-colour designs found on mid-century political posters, like President Eisenhower's 'I Like Ike' campaign, inspired this series of advertising posters for the Oakland A's. The designers wanted to create the impression that the team's star players were campaigning for fan loyalty.

Right **Mark Denton Design, Merrydown Cider Poster. Client: Merrydown Cider** Mark Denton was commissioned by David Dye to design a poster for the Merrydown Vintage brand as part of a long-running award-winning campaign. The brief required that the poster have a period feel to reflect the 'vintage' aspect of the product. The solution is a playful homage to the 1920s film *Metropolis* with an added hint of 1950s B movie.

Efrat Rafaeli Design, 'Byproduct' catalogue and exhibition announcement. Client: Southern Exposure The 'Byproduct' exhibition posed questions about the function, aesthetics and impetus of the design process and its traditional applications. The designer saw this as being central to her solution. Rafaeli states that '… the catalogue serves as a design commentary on the gimmickry and cliches of this commercial discipline. The loose coupon-like cards are packed in a zip-lock bag, and printed with bold colours, screaming for attention. A star-burst sticker with an exclamation point calls for attention, but delivers no concrete promises.' She goes on to say that '… many of the design elements that were used in this piece, such as: the star-burst, exclamation point, colour gradients, a collection of display fonts, and the use of other common dingbats became widely popular during the fifties, an era which saw the birth of branding and mass-market advertising. This vernacular iconography is still widely employed today, which makes the catalog look both retro and current at the same time.'

Left **GBH, D&AD The Clinic. Client: British Design & Art Direction (D&AD)** D&AD is a charitable organization with the mission to foster and support the next generation of creativity both in Britain and internationally. D&AD's 'Yellow Pencil' is an award which represents the pinnacle of achievement in the creative industries. GBH designed the direct-mail elements for an education initiative called The Clinic, where advertising and design agencies pledge involvement to individual colleges via differing levels of commitment: 'This could include talks, part-time teaching, work placements and sponsorships. The 1960s Pop Art-inspired badges served as a kind of contract between educators and industry representatives and were sent out by direct mail with the invitation.'

Below left **Mucca Design, Su-Zen Invitation. Client: Su-Zen** Established in Chicago, Su-Zen is a fashion company that specializes in handmade tailored knits and classically tailored clothing. When Su-Zen opened a shop in New York, Mucca Design were commissioned to build a brand identity and design a range of branded communications. The designers recount how the 'logo grew naturally out of the company's reputation for handmade, hand-tailored fashion and is designed to resemble a traditional tailor's label. For the grand opening of the new store we created a woven tailor's label the size of a postcard to serve as the invitation'.

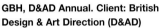

GBH, D&AD Annual. Client: British Design & Art Direction (D&AD)

GBH designed the fortieth annual, show reel, call-for-entries campaign, advertising and associated materials for the 2002 D&AD awards. To avoid a rich tradition of 'pencil'-themed annuals, GBH sought inspiration in the gold and silver of the D&AD Awards and created a concept of 'shining achievement'. This concept was applied across a range of applications. The annual cover was given a yellow 'duster' dustjacket. The gold and silver awards were subverted as 1950s Brasso-inspired polish tins. In addition, a host of press ads were designed for different territories, each one featuring a previous Gold Award winner 'endorsing' the competition in a playful homage to 1950s advertising.

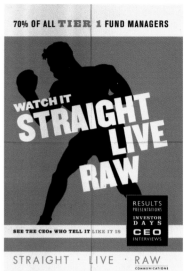

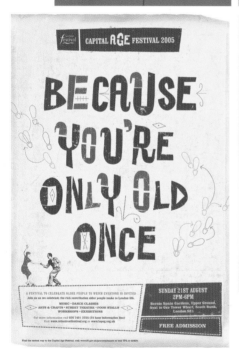

Above **Unreal, press advertising.
Client: Raw Communications**
Designed to promote real-time broker
debates online, this press campaign uses
the graphic vocabulary of boxing posters
as a play on the perceived aggressive
nature of brokers.

Left **Unreal, Capital Age Festival
posters. Client: Greater London
Authority** These posters for the Capital
Age Festival, a celebration of London's
mature population, use the styles familiar
to the target audience in their youth.

Opposite **Morla Design, *San Francisco
2012*: US Olympic bid city poster.
Client: Bay Area Sports Organizing
Committee** The Bay Area Sports
Organizing Committee chose Morla
Design to create a poster to publicize
San Francisco as the US bid city for
the Summer 2012 Olympic Games.
The designers created a contemporary
version of the photomontage style
associated with modernism that
'incorporated the optimism of the
Olympics and a bold, iconic portrait
of an Asian American swimmer. The
radiating lines, bright colour palate, and
posterized dot screens are a modern
take on San Francisco music posters
from the 1960's'.

SAN FRANCISCO
2012

Resources

General

Bagnall, G., 'Consuming the Past', in
S. Edgell, K. Hetherington and A. Warde,
(eds), Consumption Matters:
The Production and Experience of
Consumption, Oxford, 1997
Connerton, P., How Societies Remember,
Cambridge, 1989
Davis, F., Yearning for Yesterday: A
Sociology of Nostalgia, London, 1979
Hobsbawm, E., and T. Ranger, The
Invention of Tradition, Cambridge, 1992
Jameson, F., 'Postmodernism, or
The Cultural Logic of Late Capitalism',
in T. Docherty (ed.), Postmodernism:
A Reader, London, 1993
Middleton, D., and D. Edwards (eds),
Collective Remembering, London, 1990
Tannock, S., 'Nostalgia Critique', Cultural
Studies 9/3, 1995, pp. 453–64

The History of Graphic Design and
Stylistic Surveys

Aynsley, J., Pioneers of Modern
Graphic Design: A Complete History,
London, 2004
Baines, P., Penguin by Design: A Cover
Story 1935–2005, London, 2005
Blackwell, L., 20th Century Type,
London, 2004
Heller, S., and S. Chwast, Graphic Style:
From Victorian to Digital, New York, 2001
Heller, S., and L. Fili, Stylepedia: A Guide
to Graphic Design Mannerisms, Quirks
and Conceits, San Francisco, 2006
Heller, S., and M. Ilíc, Icons of Graphic
Design, London, 2001
Heller, S., and E. Pettit, Graphic Design
Timeline: A Century of Milestones, New
York, 2000
Hollis, R., Graphic Design: A Concise
History, London, 2001
Livingston, A. and I., The Thames and
Hudson Dictionary of Graphic Design
and Designers, London, 2003
McQuiston, L., The Graphic Design
Sourcebook, London, 1987
Meggs, P., A History of Graphic Design,
New Jersey, 2006
Opie, R., Packaging Sourcebook,
London, 1989
Remington, R., American Modernism:
Graphic Design 1920–1960, London,
2003

Timmers, M. (ed.), The Power of the
Poster, London, 1998
Weill, A., Graphics: A Century of Poster
and Advertising Design, London, 2004
—, Graphic Design: A History,
New York, 2004
Woodham, J., A Dictionary of Modern
Design, Oxford, 2004
—, Twentieth Century Design, Oxford,
1997
—, Twentieth Century Ornament,
London, 1990

Retro, Nostalgia and Memory in
Design and Material Culture

Bierut, M., W. Drenttel, S. Heller and
D. K. Holland (eds), Looking Closer:
Critical Writings on Graphic Design, New
York, 1994
Heller, S., 'History Lite', in The Graphic
Design Reader, New York, 2002
—, 'Through the Past Knowingly', Voice:
AIGA Journal of Design, May 2005
—, and G. Anderson, New Vintage Type:
Classic Fonts for the Digital Age, London,
2007
—, and J. Lasky, Borrowed Design: The
Use and Abuse of Historical Form, New
York, 1993
Heward, T., 'Revivalism and Cultural
Shift: British Graphic Design since 1945',
Design Issues 15/3, 1999
Meggs, P., 'The Age of Information:
Graphic Design in the Global Village:
Postmodern Design', in A History of
Graphic Design, New York, 2006
Meikle, J. L., 'A Paper Atlantis:
Postcards, Mass Art and the American
Scene', Journal of Design History 13/4,
200, pp. 267–286
Poynor, R., 'Appropriation', in
No More Rules: Graphic Design and
Postmodernism, London, 2003
Weiss, E., 'Packaging Jewishness:
Novelty and Tradition in Kosher Food
Packaging', Design Issues 20/1, 2004,
pp. 48–61

Design and Material Culture

Guffey, Elizabeth E., Retro:
The Culture of Revival, London, 2006
Jens, H., 'Sixties Dress Only! The
Consumption of the Past in a Retro
Scene', in A. Palmer, H. Clark (eds),

Old Clothes, New Looks: Second Hand
Fashion, Oxford, 2005
Kwint, M., C. Breward and J. Aynsley
(eds), Material Memories, Oxford, 1999
Radley, A. 'Artefacts, Memory and a
Sense of the Past', in D. Middleton et al.
(eds), Collective Remembering,
London, 1990
Samuels, R., 'Retrochic', in Theatres of
Memory, London, 1994
Stewart, S., On Longing: Narrative of the
Miniature, the Gigantic, the Souvenir, the
Collection, Baltimore, 1984
Woodham, J., 'Nostalgia, Heritage and
Design', in Twentieth Century Design,
Oxford, 1997

Picture acknowledgments

Archivio Depero; Atelier David Smith, www.atelier.ie; Saul Bass: courtesy of the Academy of Motion Picture Arts and Sciences and Jennifer Bass; Ivan Chermayeff and Tom Geismar, Chermayeff & Geismar; © Condé Nast Publications Inc.; Doyle, Dane, Bernbach, DDB New York; Eduardo Garcia Benito / Vogue, © Condé Nast Publications Inc.; copyright The Estate of Edward Bawden and Fortnum & Mason; Mary Evans Picture Library; Ken Garland; Milton Glaser; Grapus, 1975; Armin Hofmann; IBM; Alastair Keady, www.hexhibit.com; Typefaces courtesy of Linotype GmbH, www.linotype.com; Robert Opie Collection; Elaine Lustig Cohen; NKF, N.V. Nederlandsche Kabelfabriek Delft; Olivetti UK Ltd., Otto and Marie Neurath Isotype Collection, © University of Reading; P22 Type Foundry; Pentagram Design; Pink Floyd; original artwork © Jamie Reid 1977; Seymour Chwast, Pushpin Studio; The Tschichold family (Switzerland); www.veer.com; Victoria & Albert Museum, Barry Warner; © Marion Wesel-Henrion; the Westinghouse logo is a registered trademark of Westinghouse Electric Corporation and is used with permission; Lance Wyman

Every effort has been made to trace the copyright owners of the images contained in this book and we apologize for any unintentional omissions. We would be pleased to insert an appropriate acknowledgement in any reprint of this publication.

Contacts

Allies
alliesdesign.com
Ashby Design
ashbydesign.com
Atelier David Smith
atelier.ie
Atelier Poisson
atelierpoisson.ch
Atelier Works
atelierworks.co.uk
Andreu Balius
andreubalius.com
Jonathan Barnbrook
barnbrook.net
Base Design
basedesign.com
Billie Jean
billiejean.co.uk
Build
designbybuild.com
Cahan & Associates
cahanassociates.com
Austin Carey
careydermody.com
Alison Carmichael
alisoncarmichael.com
DDB Dallas
tribalddb.com
DDFH&B
ddfhb.ie
Mark Denton Design
markdentondesign.com
Design Factory
designfactory.ie
Designworks Enterprise IG
designworkseig.com
Dogo
undogo.com
Michal Doret
michaeldoret.com
The Foundry
foundrytypes.co.uk
GBH
gregorybonnerhale.com
Carin Goldberg Design
caringoldberg.com
HarrimanSteele
harrimansteel.co.uk
Hatch Show Print
hatchshowprint.com

Headcase Design
headcasedesign.com
Hoefler & Frere-Jones
typography.com
Image Now
imagenow.ie
Haley Johnson Design
hjd.com
Kesselskramer
kesselskramer.nl
Nils Leonard
nilsleonard.com
Malone Design
malonedesign.co.uk
Peter Mendelsund
mendelsund.com
Morla Design
morladesign.com
Mucca Design
Muccadesign.com
Laura Meseguer
laurameseguer.com
Lewis Moberly
lewismoberly.com
NB: Studio
nbstudio.co.uk
Odm Oficina
odmoficina.com
Fabio Ongarato Design
fodesign.com.au
Oxide Design Co.
oxidedesignco.com
Paprika
paprika.com
Parallax Design
parallaxdesign.com.au
Pearlfisher
pearlfisher.com
Alejandro Paul
sudtipos.com
Peguin
penguin.co.uk
Pentagram
pentagram.com
Paul Rogers Studio
paulrogersstudio.com
Reach
reachdesign.co.uk
Sandstrom Design
sandstromdesign.com
Sid Lee
sidlee.com

David Pearson
davidpearsondesign.com
Felix Sockwell, Inc.
felixsockwell.com
Spunk
spkdm.com
Spur Design
spurdesign.com
Strichpunkt
strichpunkt-design.de
Templin Brink Design
templinbrinkdesign.com
Efrat Rafaeli Design
efratrafaelidesign.com
The Designers Republic
thedesignersrepublic.com
The Marlin Company
marlinco.com
The Remingtons
theremingtons.ch
The Small Stakes
thesmallstakes.com
The Stone Twins
thestonetwins.com
Third Eye Design
thirdeyedesign.co.uk
Together Design
togetherdesign.co.uk
Alex Trochut
alextrochut.com
Una (Amsterdam) designers
unadesigners.nl
Underware
underware.nl
Unreal
unreal-uk.com
vasava
vasava.es
Jill von Hartmann Graphic Design
jvhdesign.com
Werner Design Werks
wdw.com
Williams Murray Hamm
creatingdifference.com